parallel logic

a memoir
A New Yorker's take
on life in an Eskimo
village

Elise Sereni Patkotak

All rights reserved. No part of this book may be reproduced in whole or part or any form, stored in a retrieval system or transmitted in any form without the prior written permission of the author. Permission is granted for "fair use": brief excerpts in book reviews, newspapers, magazines, news letters and online publications.

parallel
logic
A Memoir
A New Yorker's take
on life in an Eskimo village

Published by
Precious Cargo, Ltd.
Anchorage, Alaska
e-mail: TheParrot@aol.com
www.ElisePatkotak.com

Copyright © 2001 by Elise Sereni Patkotak

ISBN: 978-1-57833-445-2

Printed in the United States of America
through **Alaska Print Brokers**, Anchorage, Alaska.

Cover Design: Bob Paulson
Cover Photo courtesy of Noe Texeira

Distributed exculsively by:

Todd Communications
611 E. 12th Ave.
Anchorage, Alaska 99501-4603
(907) 274-8633 (TODD) Fax: (907) 929-5550
with other offices in Ketchikan, Juneau, Fairbanks and Nome Alaska
sales@toddcom.com • **WWW.ALASKABOOKSANDCALENDARS.COM**

To Charles Dickens; His description of
Mr. Pickwick ice-skating taught me that
books can make you laugh out loud.

TABLE OF CONTENTS

Chapters

1	Parallel Logic Meets The North	9
2	Adeline: A Parrot Meets The Arctic	15
3	The Arctic Night: A Love Affair to Remember	23
4	The Queensberry Rules of Combat Card Games	29
5	Arctic Squatting Rules And Other Cold Weather Camping Hints	39
6	The Arctic Waltz – A Quick Two Step	49
7	FelAir – An Airline You Can Trust	57
8	You Lost A What?!!!	71
9	The Tyrannosaurus Rex Mosquito And Other Arctic Summer Phenomena	87
10	Gas Toilets: The Flames That Burn The Brightest!	95
11	Your Holiday Operator Loves You	101
12	Cabin Fever – The Heat That Holds No Warmth	107
13	Cheese Bar Anyone?	117
14	Cabinets – Small Rooms On A Cruise Ship	131
15	Polar Bears Go First	139
16	The Midnight Sun Snowball Tournament	147

Chapters continued

17 Adeline – She Never Met A Man She Didn't Like   159

18 And The Winner is . . .   169

19 Everyone's From Somewhere Else   179

20 We Are Not Barren   187

⫸ PARALLEL LOGIC ⫷

Chapter 1

Parallel Logic meets the North

In 1972, while living in New York City, the man I was ready to embrace for life left me. He left me for someone named Pedro. Not knowing quite how to react, I decided to leave town. If I remember correctly, my rationale went something like this:

He left me. I'll go as far away as possible to the most inhospitable place on earth that has human habitation and a grocery store. I'll be utterly miserable and unhappy. That'll make him sorry.

It's that kind of logic that's dominated my life. In some cases, it's resulted in interesting encounters between the IRS and me (No, sir, I really DID think he had invested my money legally.) In other cases it has led to some interesting life choices (Why, Professor? You ask why am I a biology major? Why because I make A's too easily in English. In biology, I have to struggle for a C. Ergo, biology must be a much more important subject.)

In the end though, the one exceptionally interesting result of this thinking – thinking I refer to as parallel logic – is that it got me on a plane to Barrow at a time when I was quite convinced that Little Joe Cartwright was the only thing that stood between civilization (all of which occurred east of the Mississippi) and the savagery of the Wild West. Parallel logic, by the way, is when it sounds right without ever actually touching reality.

The summer my love so unceremoniously dumped me, I'd been living and nursing in New York City for four years. I knew nursing was the one career that could sweep me away to any glamorous port of call I chose because – as my parents so often told me – people will always need nurses, so you'll always have a job. This is certainly true, though I wonder if it was the brightest line of reasoning to follow as I decided what to do with the rest of my life. Parallel logic had struck again.

When I suddenly found myself without any long-term commitments, I decided to check out that first port of call. Being young and passionate, I was reasonably certain I'd never love again so I might as well go on to something else. I grabbed my latest copy of the American Journal of Nursing and flipped to the ads in the back. I had certain criteria for my selection. I didn't want to be somewhere with many bugs or snakes. And I wanted to remain absolutely miserable so HE'D be sorry about what HE'D done to me.

Not surprisingly, right up there in the A's was an ad for nurses to work in remote Alaskan villages in Federal Indian Health Service hospitals. Well, it sounded like bugs and snakes wouldn't be a problem. And it was a government job. Another axiom in my family's liturgy about the working life was, "Get a civil service job. You'll always have job security." Here was a chance to combine two opportunities at job security into one – I'd be a nurse AND have a government job. On top of that, it certainly seemed capable of fitting the requirement that I be absolutely the most miserable I could be short of cohabiting with bugs and snakes.

I chose Barrow as my destination for a very simple reason. When the recruiter called in response to my inquiry, he listed a series of available locations to see if any might be of particular interest to me. Barrow was the only name even slightly familiar though I couldn't quite remember why. After choosing Barrow, I hung up and checked it out in the atlas. Darned if the name wasn't familiar because I had studied it in fourth grade geography as the farthest north village in the United States. Well, at least that was proof positive that Alaska was indeed a state.

I gave myself six weeks to move after accepting the job. It sounded like plenty of time to unload an apartment full of cast off furnishings, say goodbye to every friend and relative I ever knew, quit my job, figure out how to transport a parrot across state lines and make sure HE knew what HE'D done to me.

Telling my family about the impending move proved a little more difficult. Ever since my grandparents had emigrated from Italy in the early 1900's, my family considered a move of anything greater than a sixty-mile radius from Center City Philadelphia as a leap into the dark abyss. You were mourned when you left and welcomed back as a hero when you returned. My Aunt Louise received this treatment when, in the 1920's, she moved to Brooklyn after she married. My mother felt this way when moved by my father from Philadelphia to Atlantic City – a move that barely qualified under the radius rule. I'd received that reaction when I moved to New York City. I couldn't begin to imagine what the reaction would be to Alaska.

Since I've always been a pro at figuring out the best time and place to make earth shattering announcements, I waited till the family was gathered together at a wedding, sitting around waiting for the Red Dye #5 roast beef to be served. I must compliment my mother. Ever the lady, she did not react violently to the news though I'm not sure she'll ever face a roast beef dinner with neutral emotions again.

I left for Alaska on October 1, 1972. I was accompanied to the airport by a large contingent of relatives who seemed unduly concerned that this move would somehow lead to my permanent removal from their circle. Although in hindsight that proved more true than not, at the time I found myself wondering if my grandparents had had to endure this when they departed for America. Of course, at that point I wasn't too sure the move was as bright an idea as it had seemed when first conceived. Some things are much cloudier in the light of stark reality than they are in the much dimmer glow cast by parallel logic.

My most vivid memory of that day occurred when I checked my beloved parrot Adeline into cargo. She was stuffed into what she considered a very small carrying cage considering the more gracious accommodations she'd grown so used to. She was clearly unhappy at the prospect of being the first tropical bird in the arctic. And she'd unfortunately picked up some language in her time with me – though I have absolutely no idea who could have taught it to her – that was very expressive of these feelings. I don't think even death will wipe out the picture I have of her carrying cage flowing on the conveyor belt back to the cargo area while she let loose with some of her more scatological expressions in a voice that could be heard in Chicago. Airline staff and customers were popping out of every nook and cranny imaginable to see exactly who was creating this cacophony of four letter words. I was beating a hasty retreat up the escalator trying to pretend I had no connection with the scene. Every time I surreptitiously glanced down at the counter area, I'd find three or four hands pointing to me.

I think my plane trip that day could be most simply described by stating that I cried all the way from New York to Alaska. In between, I tried to force my way into the cockpit in a vain attempt to get the plane to turn around. If I recollect properly, we hadn't even hit Cleveland before it occurred to me that I'd made a fairly horrible mistake.

I arrived in Anchorage a very long lifetime later. I couldn't believe how many hours it had taken me to get there. I found it even harder to believe that I still had to fly three more hours to get to Barrow. Surely I would fall off the edge of the earth long before that happened.

A member of the Indian Health Service staff picked me up in Anchorage. He drove me to the Native Medical Center and dropped me off at "quarters". Quarters housed transient staff as well as patients and families in from the Bush for medical treatment. Two rooms were connected by a common bath. Your assignment was the luck of the draw. There was no separation of patient, staff or patients' families.

As I checked in at the front desk, the receptionist leaned forward and whispered that she would recommend keeping my door to the bathroom locked at all times since "You never know who's going to be put in the next room . . . if you know what I mean." Well, that certainly calmed me down and made me feel better.

I got to the room, put down my very unhappy parrot, securely locked the bathroom door and sobbed for another hour. Then I sat up and tried to figure out how I could quickly depart on the next plane for New York without breaking my federal contract. I think that night was one of the longest in my life. I know it was for Adeline. Not only was she still in a cramped, uncomfortable carrying cage, but also I think she suspected I planned to put her back in the belly of one of those really big birds again.

The next day I was treated to the IHS version of orientation. I was trotted around to every office in the medical center so I could meet the people who were support staff for the Bush hospitals. Since I'd never worked for government before, and had no idea what Indian Health Service was actually all about, the day was only minimally useful. In fact, when it ended, I still had no idea why it had even occurred. From the vantage point of twenty years later, I think it was just a ploy to give me a break before Barrow.

Sometime in the late afternoon, the Director of Nursing decided that I should go to the local Army Navy store and get some arctic gear. Clearly what I considered a winter coat in the lower '48 would not work in the Arctic except in summer. The Director told me I should get this stuff before heading "up north". Silly me. I already thought I was up north!

I bought the standard issue green parka that seemed to be Alaska's official uniform. I also purchased matching boots and gloves. I remember thinking I was going to look like a mercenary in camouflage when I suited up. At the time, I was unaware that so would everyone else.

Early the next morning I left for Barrow on one of the three planes a week that flew there. The route followed then still applies. You fly to Fairbanks, Barrow and Prudhoe Bay/Deadhorse and then back to Fairbanks and on to Anchorage. It's the circle that can't be broken, though to break the monotony you occasionally fly to Prudhoe first before heading to Barrow. Once you cross the Brooks Range north of Fairbanks, the land starts looking very flat and very white except for a few months in the summer when it looks very flat and greenish brown, dotted with a thousand lakes. This is the north slope of the Brooks Range and it is tundra till you hit the sea.

Since pipeline activity at Prudhoe Bay was just beginning, that area was not yet served by direct flights. The only flights going there went through Barrow. Not knowing this then, I found myself shrinking back in my seat while trying to guess why I was the only female on board. I also seemed to be the only person not trying to work up to, or get over, a very bad hangover. Later someone explained that I'd flown up with pipeline workers.

In the early seventies, facilities at Deadhorse were fairly primitive and shifts were pretty long. The men who worked there worked hard, seven days a week for several weeks in a row. They played just as hard when they got their R & R time. They'd hit the nearest city with a huge wad of bills and a roaring thirst for women and drink. Considering the size of the bills they carried, they were usually successful in finding both in Fairbanks.

Trying to get service on one of these flights was quite interesting if you were female. Any flight carrying over thirty men who had been working in primitive conditions for over six weeks without benefit of women or any civilizing influence should be a flight restricted only to those security personnel necessary to complete it safely. Others placed their sanity and generally good disposition at risk.

Since your seatmate on any given flight was apt to be one of these oil field workers, you found yourself on the receiving end of many, various offers. Some involved drinks and some involved heavier commitments. Inevitably, if you turned down the drink, your seatmate took it very personally. And nothing less than seizures in the aisle would bring you to the attention of the stewardesses who were vying to see who could serve the most alcohol in the eighty minutes it took to fly from Prudhoe to Fairbanks. Frequently your coffee was served as the plane was landing.

But on that brisk October 3 morning, I was unaware this flight was not an aberration but typical of many flights I'd be taking in the future. I flew in the blissful ignorance so necessary to getting us through those times in our lives when we have no choice but to continue down a chosen path – no matter how crazy the choice now seemed.

Chapter 2

Adeline: a Parrot meets the Arctic

I arrived in Barrow about noon. This was good because it got me in during some of the few daylight hours left. By the end of November, the sun would set one last time not to be seen again until the end of January. The plane landed and taxied up to a small hut. This hut was, in turn, surrounded by a lot of other small sheds, shacks and huts. I remember wondering how far it was to town. I also remember being a little puzzled about exactly where the terminal building was. Then I saw the small sign on the side of the hut on the runway. Gosh darn if that wasn't the terminal. With no room for a baggage area, all bags were placed in the snow near a railing.

As I slowly left the plane – for some reason I was having trouble getting my hand to loosen its grip on the door – the horrible thought entered my mind that perhaps town was not as far away as I suspected. That, in fact, I was already in town. As Judy Garland once said, "I don't think we're in Kansas anymore, Toto".

Gathered around the baggage railing was a group of people from the hospital. I'd spoken to them on the phone in an interview prior to making a final commitment to the position. At the time of the interview, I thought I'd be very lucky if they actually accepted me considering the rather tentative silence that greeted my announcement that I'd be accompanied by a tropical bird. I was blissfully unaware of the fact that they'd been short of nurses for almost six months. About the only criteria applied to my hire was whether I was breathing. The interview having resolved this, they'd had no further questions.

Everyone waved madly to me. It was one of the warmest welcomes I've ever received. Since I was still unaware of the true circumstances, I thought how different this warmth was from the more distant attitude of New York. For a brief moment, I thought that maybe Barrow wouldn't be so bad after all.

I entered the "terminal" to find a scene that quickly dispelled any optimism that dared to rear its ugly head in my dark soul. On the floor of the room was Adeline's cage. She was, if possible, even more annoyed than she'd been when we arrived in Anchorage. Only at this point she felt completely uninhibited about expressing her displeasure. I don't know what pushed her over the edge. Maybe it was the first feel of an Arctic autumn when they got her out of cargo and into the hut. Maybe 20-degree weather is just something parrots don't appreciate.

Whatever caused her to snap, she went with a vengeance. There she sat in her little travel box, surrounded by a large group of stunned oil field workers. From her beak poured a steady stream of words that marked her as an honor graduate of the School for the Scatologically Advanced. The hospital staff stopped dead in their tracks. I sensed the tiniest edge of regret that they'd not stiffened the hiring criteria.

Because I have to go to the bathroom whenever there is a crisis – something that made me an interesting ER nurse – I pretended Adeline must be someone else's parrot and asked for the bathroom. The warning looks shared by the staff should have told me something. But I couldn't hear it over the steady stream of obscenities emanating from my pet. Finally, I heard the doctor, Ose Matsutani, say, "Let her go. She'll have to learn sometime." Since I'd long ago figured out how to properly perform certain bodily functions, I was puzzled as to what I'd have to learn. But I had to go badly enough to ignore him.

I entered a room – and I use the word advisedly – in which there was a throne. No, not "a throne" as in a euphemism for toilet, but throne as in a raised platform with big seat in the middle. The odor wafting towards me was one that would become hauntingly familiar over the next twenty years – the smell of Pine Sol mixed with . . . well, let's just say, mixed with other stuff. I mounted the throne gingerly and lifted the lid. I would later find out that what I'd encountered for the first time was a giant size version of the "honeybucket".

Until that moment, I'd never really given much thought to plumbing. I just assumed it would be wherever I went in these United States in basically the same form. I'd yet to encounter the benign neglect of the Federal Government towards its own Native people. While the government poured billions of dollars into foreign aid programs, most Native Americans had plumbing on par with Third World countries. A honeybucket was, and is, the only form of toilet available in most of Arctic Alaska.

So here I was, three days out of New York City, my parrot sitting in the middle of a shed in the Arctic screaming obscenities that made oil field workers blush, and I was faced with the choice of using the available facility or simply dying right then and there. I chose life, but only barely.

No one said much about what I'd just encountered when I emerged. Everyone who moves to the Bush from Outside has their own first memory of their encounter with honeybuckets. Most of us file it away under the heading "You Had To Be There" and get on with our lives.

We left the terminal and got aboard a strange vehicle called a "manhaul" – or, as one of our more progressive nurses insisted, "Allhaul". It was a truck that had been fitted with airplane tires, a cabin built on its flat bed and little to no brakes. The driver's seat was frozen in a position at some distance from the pedals making it a challenge to reach them for any purpose. Dr. Matsutani – who today might be termed vertically challenged – was often seen heading inexorably into the wall of the hospital while pumping frantically on the non-existent brakes and a clutch that he could barely reach. Thankfully the overblown airplane tires hit the wall about the same time as the fender and caused a gentle, only slightly jarring stop. Ose would then jump out and saunter off as though this was exactly where he'd planned to park.

As the Allhaul pulled away from the terminal, I peered anxiously out the small cutout in the back door of the truck bed's cabin. What I saw certainly seemed challenging. The "houses" were, for the most part, small huts made of wood from any crate available. It was not till later that it would dawn on me that since we were above the Arctic Circle, wood would be a fairly scarce commodity and so every scrap, even driftwood, was cherished and recycled. The Inupiaq – for such was the name of the Eskimo group with whom I was about to make my home – were nothing if not recycling conservationists long before recycling became politically correct.

The roads were unpaved – gravel, snow and ice mixed to make a reasonably acceptable surface for walking, skidooing, biking, ice-skating and driving. There were no street signs, no traffic signs and no traffic except for the occasional roar of a skidoo. Main routes were fairly well defined while others were barely discernible paths between houses. Houses sat in every direction and every possible position on any given block. There were no sewage or water hookups. Only a few people had telephones though most had electricity. The total population was about 2900.

The pipes that brought gas into homes for heat were laid across fifty-gallon drums that had been crushed down and placed at set intervals around and in between the houses. This above ground system leaked like a sieve. Whenever the pipes encountered an intersection at the end of the block, a wooden frame had been built up, over and down the other side of the intersection with the pipe following its contours. Most houses had blocks of ice sitting outside the door. When water was needed for cooking or eating, you hacked off a piece, carried it in and chipped it into a container. When you ran out of ice, you went to the fresh water lake or pack ice to get more.

The pack ice is a permanently frozen sea of ice in the Arctic Ocean. It contains chunks of crystal blue ice that have been naturally desalinized by the sun over many years. It is delicious drinking water.

The Allhaul pulled into the hospital's front yard and I entered my new home. I'd been assured that despite the rather primitive conditions in the community, both the Indian Health Service (IHS) Hospital and the Bureau Of Indian Affairs (BIA) School next door had running water and flush toilets in all its staff housing. When I first heard the local people refer to the hospital/school complex as the "Ivory Tower" I understood why. In Barrow in 1972, you could shower and flush a toilet only if you were white.

PARALLEL LOGIC

Immediately inside the front of the hospital, I saw a sign strung across the top of the stair landing. It said, "Welcome, Elise". As I passed under it, it was torn down and three nurses left in the plane from which I had just disembarked for well-deserved vacations. In an effort to be somewhat gentle, the Director of Nurses (DON), Ruth Humphreys, told me to take the rest of the day off to unpack and get familiar with the town. I was to report for duty the next day. She led me to an apartment that was quite lovely except for one little thing – none of my belongings were in it. I'd been assured by the moving company that they would arrive before I did. When I told this to Ose and Ruth, they exchanged sympathetic glances and quietly informed me I'd be lucky to see the stuff in six weeks.

While I had packed enough uniforms to survive that long, Adeline was another story. I couldn't picture her being happy in a small carrying cage for the next six weeks. However, I could see her destroying the whole apartment in that time. Unhappy parrots can vent their anger in devious ways. She'd once spent an entire night eating my boyfriend's shirt and then revisiting it all over his rug. Now, not only was she still livid over her status as baggage during our journey, but there was no relief in sight from her tiny, cramped quarters. I sensed problems ahead.

In actual fact, Adeline pretty much contained her vengeance to eating my shower curtain. The bathroom seemed the only sensible place to let her live while we waited for our belongings. She used the curtain bar for her perch. I placed her food and water in dishes on the bathtub rim. It made cleaning up easier. I just washed everything down the drain. Of course, it also made for some very interesting morning showers. She'd usually choose that time to vocally express what she thought of her new accommodations. In case I wasn't paying attention, she'd wait till my hair was full of shampoo and my hands were busy washing it and then make darting little forays onto my shoulders and arms. She'd take a healthy nip and retreat squawking to the shower curtain rod while I flailed madly about teaching her all kinds of new phrases.

By the time my stuff arrived, Adeline had become the talk of the town for many reasons. For instance, there was the moment I was forced to ask Ose to come up and check out what was happening to her bottom. I could see something hanging out of it and figured she had eviscerated herself in her anger. But no, it was just an undigested piece of shower curtain. Since there were no vets within 700 miles, Ose had the thrill of reaching up and pulling this piece of plastic out of her butt while I held her and she screeched. Undeterred by this little setback, she still proceeded to devour the rest of the curtain.

Another incident that added to her reputation occurred within days after our arrival. One of the hospital maintenance men came to my apartment to fix the bathroom sink. Ralph Aveoganna was Inupiaq and big tropical birds had probably not been foremost on his mind at any given time in his life. Unaware that anything lurked on the shower curtain with which he needed to be concerned, Ralph went directly to his task under the sink. Adeline apparently watched this whole scene in utter silence. She was waiting for just the right moment to announce her presence. Soon after Ralph positioned himself on his back looking up at the pipes, she said "Hello".

He bolted up and smashed his head on the pipes. Even worse, he crawled out from under the sink to see who was talking to him and couldn't find anyone around. Then she said "hello" again. Up to that time he was pretty sure – the bathroom being as small as it was – that whoever was calling him had to be outside the room. And certainly their voice should come from much lower down. He decided discretion was the better part of valor and fled.

Eventually, when he calmed down and could speak coherently again, his supervisor explained the apartment was not haunted but was, in fact, inhabited by a talking bird. He finished the plumbing in record time.

It was around this same time that Julia Segevan, a local parki maker, came to bring me a coat she'd custom made for my little cousin back east. She went to my apartment door and knocked. Adeline, being polite and always in the mood for company, called out, "Come in". She said this in an extremely eerie imitation of my voice.

Julia tried the doorknob and called out that the door was locked. To which, of course, Adeline responded "Hello! Come in." To which, of course, Julia politely responded, "I can't, the door is locked." I don't know how long this circular conversation had been going on when I came up the stairs and rounded the corner to my apartment. Julia, who at that very moment was engaged in the above-mentioned dialogue with Adeline, almost left her skin.

After that, word spread like wildfire about Adeline and I soon had a steady procession of children knocking at my door and asking if they could visit. They would come in groups of five or six and sit quietly on my couch staring at the bird, waiting for her to talk. I would stand there in a cold sweat afraid that when she did she'd be teaching them English words never heard at home.

But all that was in the future. I'd only just arrived. I had less than a day to catch my breath before starting a whole new life. And I was still one very home sick camper.

Then there was a knock at my door. Would I please get ready to go to Wainwright – a village even smaller than Barrow about ninety miles away – to get a patient who needed hospitalization? Suddenly, I was "Cherry Ames, Flight Nurse" and I didn't even like to fly.

Chapter 3

The Arctic Night: A Love Affair to Remember

Nursing in Barrow was not like anything I'd experienced in New York City. I'd trained at a major teaching hospital and was used to having a lot of doctors – from interns to specialists – as well as lab and x-ray technicians, pulmonary and physical therapists just a phone call away. In Barrow, more than 700 miles from the nearest major medical facility, we had two doctors and a lab tech who had received about two weeks training in x-ray techniques and subsequently doubled as the x-ray tech.

I remember one patient coming in with a hot appendix. We didn't have time to medevac her to Fairbanks or Anchorage. We also did not have surgical capabilities. So we turned the delivery room into an operating room, gave the patient a spinal since there was no general anesthesia, and proceeded to do an appendectomy.

One nurse stood in the delivery room in front of the doctor with a book turned to the page on how to do appendectomies. Another nurse held the door from the delivery room to the nurses' station open. Yet another nurse was on the phone at the nursing station with a surgeon from Anchorage. She periodically called out words of encouragement and advice from the Anchorage surgeon. Words like, "He said if you can't find it there, cut a little higher and to the left". I am convinced the only reason the patient – who could hear every word of our search for her appendix – did not leap off the table and trust her fate to the gods, was that her legs were numb from the spinal. That she survived and left the hospital a few days later is attributable to many things – not the least of which is the indomitable stoicism of the Inupiat people.

There was a nurse, an aide and a maintenance man on each shift. The aide was a local resident paired off with a nurse. Once paired, your shifts were always scheduled together. The nurse did all the training the aide received. Since the only paying jobs available in Barrow were either the BIA School, the IHS hospital or five miles down the road at a facility known as NARL (Naval Arctic Research Lab), there was never a shortage of people willing to take a job. The nurses' aides, maintenance men, housekeepers, kitchen, laundry and some secretarial staff were all from the community.

The hospital had thirteen beds, including its labor and delivery rooms and nursery. It also had an outpatient department. No private physician was available on the North Slope. There was no pharmacy except at the hospital. The state staffed one nurse at a Public Health Nursing Clinic. There was one IHS dentist and his practice included almost the entire 88 thousand square miles of the North Slope. That was also the population base for our hospital services. It included Barrow and four other villages.

If a patient was really sick, he was put on a flight to Anchorage. A nurse escort was sent along when needed. Since the nurses never received anything even closely resembling flight-nurse training, this was a chancy proposition at best. Not only were you unsure of what you were doing, you were usually doing it in the middle of a commercial jet with little to no proper equipment.

But the dangers and deprivations of life were more than compensated for by the warmth and closeness of the community. I was lucky that way. I got to Barrow at a time when a whole group of hospital personnel was involved with community life.

This was not necessarily a normal situation. Many doctors and nurse, as well as BIA teachers, never came out of their little "ivory towers." They went to work by way of a hallway connecting their apartment to the classroom or hospital and they went home the same way. They ordered food up on the "North Star", a cargo ship that came to Barrow once a year when the ice was out. When school was over for the year or their vacation was due, they went in a truck from their apartment to the airport without ever having their feet actually touch the ground of the community in which they lived.

PARALLEL LOGIC

I always wondered why these people even bothered to come to a place like Barrow if they didn't intend to sample the delight and intrigue of a culture so diametrically different from that in which they'd been raised.

The work at the hospital proved more rewarding than I'd imagined. In a small Eskimo village, things are not done as formally as they are in big cities. For instance, the hospital had a long, low table just in front of the nurses' station. There was a comfortable rocking chair on either side of it. A big pot of coffee was always brewing. If there were babies to be fed, you picked them up and went out to the table. People wandered by to see who was in the hospital and needed a visitor. They would almost always sit down for a cup of coffee and a visit before leaving. And if there were too many babies all hungry and crying at once, you just handed one to whoever was sitting in the chair – aide, maintenance man or visitor – and they fed him while you attended to other matters.

On Sundays after services, the minister came by with some of his flock. They went from room to room visiting with patients. The Inupiat being a basically non–verbal people, every one felt comfortable with visits that involved nothing more than sitting in almost absolute, yet companionable, silence for ten or fifteen minutes. Coming from an extremely verbal, some might even say loud, Italian family, this presented quite a cultural adjustment for me. I was starting to get used to it thanks to the numbers of children sitting silently in my apartment every night visiting Adeline. It would take a while, though, to get comfortable with it.

Sometimes the hospital visits were a bit more vocal. Upon request, the minister and visitors would break into hymns and sing for the patients. I quickly found out that singing was a major form of religious expression in the community. When someone died, a celebration was occurring, or someone just wanted an excuse to get together with friends, a "Singspiration" was organized.

Since life in the Arctic can be very harsh, I was quickly introduced to the differences in how death is handled. It didn't occur to me till the first death I encountered that there was no funeral home or undertaker in Barrow. Since planes only arrived three times a week, I doubted we waited to send the bodies out. I found out that in Barrow, families took care of their own when a death occurred. They sat at the bedside till the warmth left the body and then washed and dressed it for burial.

After this, the body was transferred to a two bed, refrigerated morgue. Since the morgue's refrigeration system had a horrible tendency to break down, our backup system was to place the covered body under a window in the back hallway and leave the window open. When the weather is zero to forty degrees below most of the year, this is a more than adequate way to handle the problem.

My second Christmas in Barrow was the first in which I really started to feel at home. Dr. Rob Burgess organized a little musical moment to accompany the Christmas party the hospital threw in the school multipurpose room for its entire staff and their families. Since musical instruments were limited, we improvised. For reasons that are not entirely clear at this moment, I ended up playing a bedpan full of chocolate turtles. The nurse's aide next to me played Christmas carols on vaginal speculums. We were all dressed in green scrub suits, which seemed especially appropriate for the Christmas season. And we were all laughing so hard we could barely belt out the tune.

My first experience going to a captain's house after a successful whale hunt also helped me feel at home. Whaling was, and still is, critical to the physical, spiritual and cultural life of the Inupiaq. The bowhead whale and the Inupiaq share their lives and destiny. The Inupiaq do not believe that they catch a whale – they believe the whale gives himself to them so that they may survive for another season. Everything about whaling – both in the spring off the edge of the pack ice and in the fall from the beaches on the edge of town – is circumscribed by ceremony and tradition. And a large part of that tradition is sharing – the cultural basis of Inupiaq life.

So when a captain is lucky enough to harvest a whale, his luck is predicated on the fact that he will now have the pride and pleasure of being able to share his good fortune with his community. He will share at the *Nalukataq* or Blanket Toss in June. He will share at his church on Thanksgiving and Christmas. He will share even as the whale is being cut up right after it has been caught. His wife boils up the fresh maktak, called *unaliq*, for his crew to eat while they work.

He will also share it the day after the whale has been completely butchered and the pieces brought back to town. His wife, the wives of his crew members, and just about anyone else who can help, spend all day and night cutting up very specific parts of the whale to be boiled and served, stewing fruit, and frying Eskimo donuts.

You know where to go to eat because there's a flag atop the captain's house indicating he's serving that day. When you arrive, you find people lined up around the block waiting for their meal.

When I went to my first feed at a captain's house, I'd only been in town a few weeks. The Public Health Nurse, Ruth Ward, invited me to go with her. I was appalled. I'd just arrived from New York City. New York is not the kind of place where you drop in on people uninvited even if you know them. Yet this lady wanted me to follow her to a house full of strangers and expect to be fed.

But she insisted it was OK so I followed. I fully expected to be greeted at the front door of the captain's house by people whose brows were arched at the rudeness I was exhibiting. I figured I'd then turn to Ruth and say, "I told you so". Only it turned out she got to say that.

We arrived at a scene of jubilantly organized chaos. Skidoos roared through the yard making multiple entrances and exits as they continued the work of bringing the whale meat to be stored in the ice cellar. An ice cellar can best be described as the Arctic version of a root cellar. It is dug straight down in the permafrost in the shape of an upside down mushroom.

Children ran around playing and laughing. Everyone's face was creased into smiles of happy anticipation and delight. I was allowed to blend into this scene as though I'd been part of it my whole life. The only time anyone treated me differently was when the servers made a special effort to explain what I was eating or made sure I had enough tea and had found the pot with the stewed fruit. Nowhere in the highest level of New York society could I have expected to find more warm and gracious manners. I felt a little part of my sadness and isolation depart to be replaced by the spreading warmth of tea, donuts, maktak and friendship.

Soon after that my love affair with the Arctic really began. The head of hospital maintenance was an old Arctic sourdough named Joe Hilderbrand Sr. He had practically built the Barrow hospital. One night after dinner, he invited me for a skidoo ride on the tundra. Having not yet been outside the environs of the village, I jumped at the chance to take a close look at what seemed to be barren, flat and forbidding.

It was a cold, clear Arctic night. I'd been told that on nights like this you could actually hear the snow settling on the tundra. A little ways out of town, Joe stopped his skidoo and turned off the motor. Having been born and bred in a city, I was unprepared for the absolute silence that greeted me when the engine died. It was absolute in a way that few things really are in this life. Joe suggested I lay out flat on his sled, look up and enjoy the night.

I followed his suggestion. I don't know if I actually heard the snow settling but I could swear I heard the gods whispering. It occurred to me that something very significant was happening. I was from the city where noise was incessant, like music in an elevator. As for stars, in the city they are distant companions at the best of times, glimpsed through the cracks in the skyline, always dimmed in their brilliance by smog and manmade lights.

But here in the Arctic, the sky was laid out for my delectation like a royal feast. I could pick and choose among constellations. I could savor one brightly winking point of light and then move slowly to the next. With the whiteness of the snow reflected in the light of the stars and moon, the world took on a strange and fascinating face.

As if on cue, the northern lights made their appearance. I first thought they were clouds forming in the sky. But they grew brighter and brighter. Soon fingers of color made wavy curtains over the stars. I was on the biggest stage in the universe and God had just dropped the curtain.

≫ PARALLEL LOGIC ≪

Chapter 4

The Queensberry Rules of Combat Card Games

Falling in love with the Arctic, however, didn't immediately erase all culture shock. Once my head started to clear from its initial entry into a world where people never locked their doors and you could walk around quite safely at 3 a.m., I looked about to find out what I could expect over my next two years of indentured servitude. One of the first things I found was that my initial suspicions were correct. Whatever my life had been to date was prelude. The ride was really just beginning.

For instance, I'd grown up with TV as a birthright. In Barrow, it didn't exist. At least, not until after I'd been there about six months.

On and off through the sixties there had been some attempt at TV in Barrow but nothing ever stuck. One problem was that we obviously weren't going to pick up any reception through antennas. TV would have to come through satellites and cable. As oil money started to flow into the state through the seventies, a network with state funding called the "Rural Alaska Television Network" (RATNET) was created. This channel would eventually show an amalgam of programming from the three major networks and occasionally PBS beamed to the Bush through satellite.

But in 1973, all we had was a man with a garage from which he played taped programming that had already made its way through many Alaska Bush communities. This meant that the programming was sometimes six weeks old before we saw it. But that really didn't matter. Time is kept differently in the Arctic. Life is more casual here. Eight-to-five jobs are rare, and the sun may be up or down for months at a time. No one watches clocks. Everyone takes the attitude that in time, all things will eventually come.

The first person in the hospital compound to break down and purchase a TV was Ose. He invited everyone to his place one Sunday afternoon to watch a showing of "The Ten Commandments."

We all arrived early in an attempt to get the best seat in the house. Food was scattered tastefully about and drinks were secured before show time so there would be no interruptions until intermission. Then the movie began. The first thing we all noticed – or at least eventually realized – was that the movie started with the middle tape. Instead of a grand overture or any credits, we were plunged into Egypt and what seemed like a lot of frogs.

Apparently, the gentleman playing the tape either had not noticed his mistake or decided there was no real use in correcting it. He let the middle reel play first, the first reel play second and finished big by actually getting the last reel to play last. We all applauded roundly though most of us were fairly lost about the plot by then. I think the frogs won.

I was soon to find out that this was not at all unusual when it came to the quality of TV coming from the "garage". On bingo nights, the TV was apt to end abruptly if the person monitoring the tape decided to go play. Sometimes they fell asleep and didn't notice when the tape ended. If that happened, someone with a telephone would call to try and wake them. Unfortunately, staff often took the precaution of taking the phone off the hook so it wouldn't disturb their nap. Eventually, they'd wake up on their own or someone who really wanted to see the end of the show would walk over and pound on the door. While at times this was annoying, it certainly made TV a more interactive sport than it was in the lower '48.

Understanding our city police force also took some adjustment on my part. The city police consisted of two or three officers. Some were professionally trained; some were not. Their equipment was – to put it mildly – limited. Since the entire City of Barrow then had a budget that didn't get out of the low five digits, just about everything from ammunition to uniforms to jail space was limited. The sole police car often didn't work. Jail consisted of one cell. This meant that anything over one arrest per night could get complicated unless the prisoners were the same sex. Since the fire and police stations occupied the same building, it was not at all unusual to find excess prisoners cuffed to the track of the water tank vehicle. The philosophy of a would-be prisoner was if you were going to get busted, do it early so you could get the cell with the cot.

Eventually, the city came up with the money to buy the police a three-wheeler – one of the original ATV's. I was working nights at the hospital then. Since there wasn't much to do at night unless an emergency arose, and since there weren't many people up then, the nursing station and the coffee pot there became the gathering place for those whose jobs required they be awake in the early morning hours.

The two cops on duty had come to the hospital for a cup of coffee and some conversation about 3 A.M. As they sat there relaxing, a call came in for them over the CB. They ran out to respond. I went to the window to watch their departure on the new three-wheeler. There they were. One was driving and one was sitting backward riding shotgun with a rifle cradled in his arms. There is no describing the look on the face of the cop riding shotgun backwards as the three-wheeler bounced and jumped over Barrow's rutted roads. He hung on for dear life. It was about then that I realized there was no place else on earth I really wanted to be.

Except for maybe the Polar Bear Theater – the only movie theater in Barrow. I was a young nurse looking for a social life. The Polar Bear became the center of much of my activity. Among other things, I was assured I'd always get to see every Shaft and Kung Fu movie made. After the movie, the "almost live" band "Harpoon" played for our dancing delight. The band earned the sobriquet "almost live" based on their rather spotty record of ever returning for the second set after their break. They had a propensity for taking their breaks rather seriously. They usually ended up seriously relaxed.

The management solved the problem of dance space by simply removing the first ten or so rows of seats from the theater. It didn't bother the movie-going set very much because the movies didn't matter. No one watched them. The sound system was such that the dialogue never seemed to belong to the movie on the screen. This is why action movies like "Shaft" were so popular. Dialogue was extraneous. And since actually listening to a movie was considered a low priority, receiving calls at the theater was no problem. Management simply turned up the lights and walked up and down the scattered aisles calling your name till you either answered or someone yelled out your location.

The dances started at 11 P.M. and went until 1 A.M. or whenever the band left the stage. In Barrow, I quickly learned, it was rude to try to pin people down to anything more exact. As far as could be determined, the music played was rock and roll. The favorite song was "Blueberry Hill". The fact that it was one of the few recognizable songs played may have had something to do with its popularity.

The ambiance of the dance was pure funk. The only dress code was that you had to wear clothes. Age was inconsequential. Fifty-yearolds shared the floor with twenty-year-olds. The really big equalizing factor was whether you could stand the decibel level. If there was one thing "Harpoon" knew for sure about music it was this: if you played loud and fast, everyone danced and no one cared what the song was.

When you tired of dancing, you sat in some of the remaining seats and watched entire relationships flourish and die during the course of an evening. Mothers looking for teens past curfew would periodically storm the place and drag their unwilling offspring out. The State Trooper periodically felt an obligation to storm the place and bust pot smokers. His arrival was usually announced by loud oinks from the back of the theater.

After the dance, you walked home with the Northern Lights as company, tired but satisfied that you'd danced till you dropped and kept abreast of all the latest romantic entanglements in one fell swoop.

Another favorite gathering place – and the only restaurant in town opened year round back then – was Al's Eskimo Cafe. There was a place called Brower's Cafe but it only opened in the summer for the tourists. It was tradition to go there at least once a season and eat a bowl of reindeer soup while listening to the tour guides' latest spiels about Barrow.

Al's Eskimo Cafe, owned and operated by Al Hopson Sr., was the really special place. It was the original highway greasy spoon translated into tundra ambiance. I wouldn't have been surprised if, after downing one of those wonderful grease soaked burgers with fries – this was before they invented cholesterol, when you were still allowed to savor the flavor that fried fat brings to food – I went out to find Route 66 going by the front door.

Since Al had some real strong affection for the hospital staff, we were often treated to an extra special meal in the back room. Al would call Ose and ask if he knew any hungry doctors or nurses. Needless to say there were always lots of volunteers. We'd all troop over to Al's back room where a feast fit for a king was laid before us. There'd be shrimp cocktail followed by shee fish, caribou and fresh salad, topped off with strawberry shortcake for dessert. Al's wife cooked while Al supervised the proceedings. The whole time you ate, Al would sip from his coffee cup – which did not necessarily contain coffee – and we'd listen to a master storyteller weave his magic as he told tales of a time when life on the North Slope was both simpler and harsher.

Al's Cafe burned down in the mid seventies. Of all events and actions that pointed to the passing of one way of life on the North Slope and the beginning of a new, this was probably the most significant. I was there the day the cafe burned down. Ammunition in the back room caught fire and kept exploding. It made quite a scene before the cafe gave up the ghost and collapsed. We have lots of restaurants in town now but none can hold a candle to Al's when it comes to sheer atmosphere.

When it was too cold to walk the three blocks to Al's, and the hospital food was too repetitive to face again, we turned to one another for company and amusement.

Barrow raised the mundane tradition of visiting neighbors to a high art form. A major part of visiting was dinner parties. With restaurants so limited, home cooked meals shared with friends became a core of your social life.

Of course, to serve food meant to shop. One of the joys of Barrow when I first arrived was the realization that there was no place to shop. In fact, in Alaska in 1972, there were few places to shop, period. The Bush situation was just an exaggeration of a statewide dearth of shopping centers. My family still suspects that one of the main attractions of Barrow for me was that I'd found the one place in the country where I wouldn't have to ever go shopping.

In Barrow in 1972, there were three stores. One was Brower's Store Number One. It was across the lagoon in a little subdivision of Barrow called Browerville. It was the quintessential general store. You could get a little of everything and a lot of nothing. If you wanted canned corn there was one size, one brand. You could also buy pots, guns, ammunition, a skidoo, skins for sewing your parka and a Coleman stove in the same small space. The freezer usually contained moose meat and frozen fish caught at nearby fish camps.

At Brower's Store Number Two in Barrow, there was a little less of everything, if that was possible, but a lot more sitting and visiting among the older men of the community. You went there to play checkers and discuss the issues of the day.

The biggest store in town was called Shontz's. The downstairs was filled with groceries and the upstairs contained everything else – material for coats, household items (if there were any), toys (if there were any), etc. Shontz's stood out mostly for the fact that they did get fresh stuff on a regular basis. Despite the fact that this fresh stuff usually tasted like it had all been cut from the same piece of cardboard, the reality was it didn't come in a can or box and had some distant relation to earth and soil that could still be detected. Therefore, it was treated like precious jewels.

When people came to town from outside, protocol demanded they arrive with bag loads of fresh fruits and vegetables if they wanted anything even remotely resembling a friendly greeting. And when fresh stuff arrived at the store, protocol demanded that your natural instinct to buy up everything in sight be curbed so that others could share in the bounty.

It became a matter of honor that when the store got fresh stuff you didn't run over and buy fifty heads of lettuce, then sit in your kitchen cackling gleefully over your cache. When word circulated in the hospital that the store had some, really good friends checked on their working comrades and took orders before heading out. It was assumed that if you had ten heads of lettuce in your cart it was because you were buying for friends.

Once you got it home, the expectation was that you'd host a dinner party centered on a big salad. This was often the high point of the social season. People gathered round limp, partially frozen celery, brown mushrooms, soggy tomatoes and always rusted lettuce and oohed and aahed as though the ambrosia of the gods was passing their lips. It was quite a sacred moment.

I eventually realized that if I intended to stay in Barrow, I would have to bulk order on the supply ship that came through once a year or pay to have goods air freighted in. This, in turn, created the challenge of where to store the stuff ordered. More than one piece of Bush furniture started as extra cases of soda that had to be placed somewhere until used. You carefully arranged the cases in your living room, added a tastefully draped cloth and called it an easy chair. Of course, once you actually needed the soda, you had to be quite creative to come up with a new arrangement of the remaining cases.

You have to be organized enough to stockpile not only commonly used goods, but also those once-a-year items. I spent part of one New Year's Eve tearing through the "children's toy drawer" in my spare room hoping to find a substitute for mascara. I figured something in a tasteful, water-soluble magic marker would work. The perfume I used that night was originally created for a fashion doll. She has bizarre taste. I felt like I was wearing a citrus fruit that had stayed too long at the fair. Had there been bees around, I'm sure they'd have pollinated me. The Alaska Bush is just not the place to be if you have allergies and need only a very specific type of perfume at 11 p.m. on New Year's Eve.

You also needed to be very sure you knew what a size 6 can actually was. If you didn't, you ended up with enough stewing tomatoes to feed Bolivia. When ordering a case of pimentos, you needed to know how many little jars came in that case. It was also wise to check ahead of time with family members to see how many pimentos they actually consumed in a year. Finally, never give jars of pimentos as wedding, anniversary or birthday gifts. Some people just don't appreciate them. And others are rude enough to laugh right in your face and then ask for the real gift.

Whenever the plane was due in, anyone not working or sleeping went down to the hut to see who was coming and going. If you were on your way out to Anchorage or Fairbanks, you were fair game for multiple requests for items not available locally. While most people were pretty compassionate about true emergency requests (I'm running out of insulin and I will lapse into a coma and die if you don't pick some up for me), other requests for those items you suddenly and impulsively decided you absolutely must have (How much space can one order of extra crispy wings take up in your carry on?) were met with a bit more hostility. So I learned how to improvise.

When the only wrapping paper for a child's birthday present was black with the words "Over The Hill" prominently emblazoned on the side, I simply stole her crayons and drew happy faces all over a brown paper bag. When I heard there was eggplant at the store, I impulsively invited six people over to try out a new recipe. Only later did I discover the eggplants available were those teeny tiny little ones that need about two dozen to equal the filling of one big one. So I substituted canned pumpkin and pretended it was supposed to taste that way.

The other habit developed in the Bush is that of being a pack rat. You never throw anything out that might have some future value – even if, for the life of you, you can't figure out what it could be. So what if the old coffeepot only made wet grinds for breakfast. It sounded right and created the illusion that there was actually something resembling hot coffee in the brown water that resulted. There was a time when that illusion was all you had to live for while you waited six weeks for its replacement. And who knew when that fender might not come in handy. Or those old skidoos and three-wheelers. Each and every one of them was a veritable paradise of almost usable spare parts.

I developed a three-part system to handle my recycling needs. When I decided an item had outlived its immediate usefulness in my home, I'd carefully bag it and place it in the back room. It would sit there for anywhere from six weeks to six years depending on how often I tripped over it. Then it was moved to my cold storage porch. It would languish there for an indeterminate amount of time while friends made increasingly pointed comments about old ladies found dead in their homes with trash stacked to the ceiling in plastic bags. Eventually, I'd be forced to choose between a rummage sale – as someone who hates crowds and shopping this was a questionable option at best – or hauling it out to the dump.

The dump functioned as the ultimate recycling center. When the hospital or school was throwing old furniture out, the maintenance truck would be followed to the dump by a procession of people hoping to get it on their sled or in the back of their truck first. When NARL was emptying its food stores and tossing outdated cases of everything from cereal to cabbage, everyone headed to the dump and shopped. At the dump, items that are my junk get transformed into someone else's treasures. Recycling in the Arctic is a time-honored tradition.

There was not a lot of outside distraction to keep you amused when you wanted to socialize in the Bush in the early seventies. You could go camping and hunting or you could go camping and fishing. In between and during, you played cards.

I firmly believe there are two distinct types of people in this world – card players and deprived souls. If you were of the latter variety and lived in the Bush in those distant days, you spent a lot of lonely nights listening to the sounds of screams, cries, arguments and relationships ending in the kitchen where the pinochle game was happening. If you wanted to play bridge instead of pinochle – and were actually brave enough to make this known – you spent an average of six months every year trying to get four people together for one game. If you were a bridge player who was in some position of authority when it came to hiring people to come to Barrow to work, the interview question of whether the potential hire played bridge was mandatory. In the case of close calls, bridge playing could tip the deck (pun fully intended) in the candidate's favor.

I played both bridge and pinochle. I learned bridge at college and pinochle at my father's knee. I was at his knee hiding from my nonna who could not believe what I'd just bid. She did not suffer fools gladly in her card game. Under those circumstances, I quickly learned how to be a good pinochle player for fear she'd reach me with the wooden spoon. Both my father and nonna were purists when it came to pinochle. They played only single deck and they played serious. To be admitted to their game was a major milestone on the rocky road to adulthood.

Then I got to Barrow and discovered double deck pinochle. It would have turned my nonna's hair gray just to hear the rules described. My favorite variation of the double deck game was called "pass four". In this version, you bid based on the fact that if you got the bid your partner would be able to pass four cards to you. Since you always assumed your partner would pass the exact cards needed for a double run – worth 120 points – the bidding would get a little outrageous. The game usually ended with a score of minus 700 to minus 900. The smaller minus won.

The other game I learned in Barrow was Snertz. It's mostly played by women around a table covered by a blanket. The blanket was very important in creating a non-slip surface since once the game got going, cards flew all over the place. The easiest way to explain Snertz is to say it's like playing solitaire except everyone has their own deck and is feeding cards into piles in the middle. The first person to get all her cards on the right piles won.

The catch, of course, is that everyone is trying to get his or her cards onto the same pile. If your ten of clubs gets there before my ten of clubs, I have to take mine back and try again. If you didn't move your hands in and out of the middle quickly enough, you risked getting them slapped silly by some of the older women. They took their Snertz very seriously and firmly believed in the old card adage, "Take no prisoners, show no mercy". They'd stand around the table poised to strike when the right card turned up. I don't think I ever won a game. The mere sight of them intimidated me. Arctic women of any age should never be underestimated.

Chapter 5

Arctic Squatting Rules and Other Cold Weather Camping Hints

Playing cards also became critical during long camping trips. When the weather outside the tent is twenty below zero, you need a way to keep distracted from the fact that sooner or later you're going to have to leave the tent to answer nature's call.

A favorite weekend for camping here is Memorial Day. This is usually the last weekend there's enough snow on the ground to make the trip with a loaded sled before the mud of tundra breakup sucks you into a black hole. It's also one of the last weekends you can go inland without risking a bath in the melting river waters. For many men here, the ice melting on the rivers is viewed as a challenge. They figure if they go across fast enough, they won't sink. This may be true for the skidoo in the front. On the sled in the back, however, you find yourself water skiing across the melting river while praying loud and fast.

The first thing I should explain about camping here is that you are either the driver – in which case you are male and on the skidoo; or you are the passenger – in which case you are female and on the sled. Riding an Eskimo sled loaded for a hunting trip inland is one of those graces acquired through long practice. The women up here make it look easy. It isn't.

Since the men pack the sleds, and don't have to sit on what they've packed, I'd often find myself perched uncomfortably on a couple of gas cans with lids and bumps sprouting in the most unfortunate of spots. The smart thing to do is watch when the sled is being packed and raise objections early. Your aim is to get something smooth, comfortable and without lumps in the place where you will be sitting for the next six hours or so.

Ignore this advice and you'll find yourself sore in very tender spots. Remember, these sleds have no springs, no cushions, nothing to buffer you as they are pulled at a rapid speed over open tundra – which, by the way, is not half as flat and smooth as it seems from the air.

Often the sled will lift completely off the ground when going over a bump only to slam down in a bone jarring manner seconds later. The way to keep from flying off when this happens is to hold on to any available rope that's been used to tie the gear down. Since hunters go out of their way to make sure they have lashed their gear tightly on the sled, these ropes will be quite secure. If they weren't, they'd never think of driving that fast.

I found myself camping a lot in the mid seventies because I'd fallen in love with, and married, an Inupiat hunter named James about three years after my arrival in Barrow. Since many of us spent more than a little part of our lives in the early and mid seventies wandering around dazed, the full impact of this step only gradually caught up with me.

For instance, it wasn't till after the wedding that I realized how much camping and guns would be a permanent part of my life. Getting used to the presence of guns in my daily life became a special challenge since I grew up on the East Coast before semiautomatics became the accessory of choice.

Every time James came home from a hunting trip, I would take his rifle or shotgun apart and hide all the pieces plus bullets and shells in different places. I felt this was the best way to ensure that no one was ever accidentally shot. Unfortunately, it also ensured that my husband damned near had apoplexy every time he tried to get his rifle ready for another trip since I frequently forgot where some of the pieces had been hidden.

I remember coming home from a camping trip with James soon after we married. We'd taken our puppy Lovey with us so that she would have unlimited room to run and romp. Unfortunately, Lovey – then and in all her seventeen succeeding years – never exhibited any sign of wanting to run and/or romp on the tundra. She was not a run and romp kind of dog. She was more of a "let me in this tent or I'll howl all night" kind of dog.

As we returned from a weekend spent trying to push her out of the tent to answer nature's call, I rode, as usual, on the sled. Lovey was curled up on my legs, her head securely tucked under my thigh so her nose wouldn't get cold. At that point, she wanted nothing more than to get home to sleep on the couch in front of the heater as God had clearly intended. Meanwhile, she was taking a tiny nap to rest up for sleeping later. I was also feeling fairly relaxed. Instead of gripping the ropes for dear life in anticipation of a bump, I was laying back in an attempt to cut the wind blowing in my face.

That's when I saw James go straight up in the air. The handlebars were his only connection with the skidoo. He had hit one major bump. When this happens and you are riding on the sled behind the skidoo, you have about three seconds before you hit the same bump. I realized during those three seconds that I had a choice to make. I could grab Lovey and try to save her or I could grab the ropes and save myself.

I guess I would have made a lousy mother. I didn't hesitate a second before I grabbed the ropes. Lovey was on her own. My last sight of her was when we hit the bump. She was turning a somersault in midair. The look on her face can only be described as stunned disbelief. She didn't even know she could do somersaults.

When we managed to slow down and turn the skidoo around to rescue her, I had horrible visions of finding her lifeless body in the snow. Instead, we found her running as fast as she could away from the skidoo. I was amazed she could run. Up till then she'd never bothered. But now, with that horrible mechanical monster climbing up her butt in an attempt to make another effort at killing her, she put on a burst of speed that would have done a greyhound proud. She clearly had no intention of ever getting back on a sled again.

Except for the remainder of the trip home, during which time I kept a chokehold on her to keep her from bolting, she never did. For the next fifteen years, the sound of a skidoo engine or the sight of a sled caused her to shiver with fright, whimper uncontrollably, and demand extra helpings of meat for dinner.

Another memorable camping trip occurred in 1975 when my sister Judy came to visit me. James and I were engaged. My family decided someone needed to officially represent them on a visit. Unfortunately, there were few volunteers. My sister Judy, a high school student still dependent on the family for such basics as food, shelter and clothing, didn't have much say in the matter. She'd be the sacrificial lamb.

She was quite good about the visit. She never flinched when the idea of a three-day camping trip came up even though she could clearly see it was snowing and blowing outside. My, my, as I look back on it now, I find it hard to believe how trusting and naive she really was.

We were going camping with my soon to be in-laws. Since they are basically kind and caring people, they went out of their way to see that Judy would be dressed warmly for this adventure. She was piled in as many clothes as physically possible while still allowing room for some movement and shallow breathing. The attire in which she was sent out to meet the Arctic elements of spring consisted of: underwear followed by long johns, three pair of socks, jeans and T shirt, flannel shirt, sweater, mouton socks, boots, ski pants, ski vest, parka, knitted cap, hood, muffler, knitted gloves and fur-lined mittens. Just as we finished layering her, the windy, snowy weather turned really bad.

If I peered very closely inside the layers, I could just make out the panic in her eyes. I wasn't sure what her greatest fear was at that point – discovering she had to go to the bathroom or finding out that she still might be cold. We completed her bundling by placing every blanket, quilt and caribou skin available on top of her. When we were done, she looked as if she could have survived a moon shot without the capsule. And she probably could have. A camping trip on the tundra would prove a bit more difficult.

For instance, there was that moment of startling clarity when she realized she might have to use nature as her outhouse since there seemed to be no conveniently placed portable facilities. She also noticed there were no trees or tall bushes. I explained to her she'd just have to go as far from camp as possible and trust that no one cared enough to look.

I'll never forget the sight of her trudging bravely off towards the distant horizon, roll of paper in hand, looking for any depression or curve in the land's surface that would give her even the illusion of privacy. She asked me to follow due to some concern about wild animals. I tried to explain to her that wild animals would be the least of her worries but she didn't believe me.

As I think back on it now, I'd venture to guess that the moment I packed her onto the sled with the snow storm whirling about was probably the last moment she had of trusting, unquestioned faith in her older sister's judgment.

Since she was walking ahead of me, she reached the top of a slight rise and crossed over and down before I got there. A few seconds later, as I crested the incline, I saw her getting ready to begin the task at hand totally oblivious to geese hunters hiding behind every clump of dirt on the rise. All were watching with quizzical interest wondering – I'm sure – why she'd come this far from camp to be so public. Luckily, I arrived in time to stop her.

Not too long after this, she found herself on a sled being pulled by a skidoo chasing a caribou. Through the wind blowing in my face as I rode clinging to the back of the sled, I could hear her screaming, "Run, you stupid caribou, run!" This was not likely to endear her to the hearts of hunters anywhere let alone the particular hunter who was trying to shoot our dinner. But she, like me, had been raised on Bambi. We'd both been traumatized by the same scene – as had most of America. The sight of Bambi standing alone in the forest calling out "Mother!" is not easily erased. Those early childhood influences can be hell to overcome.

In the end, both because she had no choice and because she wanted to be polite, she rode back to camp with a caribou lashed down to the sled in front of her. Though she was not a happy camper at that moment, she was certainly a very brave one. When hunting is not the life style in which you were raised, this kind of trip can take some getting used to – especially when a dead animal's head is bumping up and down on the sled in front of you. Especially when that animal is the nearest thing to Bambi you've ever seen so close and personal. Especially when you get back to camp and watch the beetles that live in the hide break through and start crawling around after the caribou has been dressed out.

The highlight of her trip came when my in-laws announced they wanted to go visit some old friends. Judy looked around at the white, relatively trackless land and wondered if my soon to be mother-in-law had taken leave of her senses. We took off to a house on the top of a bluff overlooking a nearby river. People had lived there year round when the nearby coal mine supplied Barrow's fuel. Only one family lived there now.

We entered a house where a turkey was roasting in the oven and a birthday cake was being decorated. The house had its own generator so there was electricity. It also had a bathroom even if the bathroom did contain a honeybucket. Judy soon found out how good they could be when your only other option is bare ground.

The ultimate inland Memorial Day camping trip occurred later in the seventies with a friend named Sam. Since I was divorced from James by then, I was not traveling with the family on their camping trips. I missed going on to the land and enjoying the springtime explosion of life there.

Despite the fact that there was still snow and cold weather, by the end of May the birds have returned to the tundra and it is alive with songs, activities and daily dramas. There is hardly a lake or pond not supporting a pair of swans. Loons sing you to sleep at night – if, indeed, their voices can be said to be singing. Ducks, owls, geese, eagles, snowbirds, and ptarmigan – the tundra holds well over two hundred and fifty different kinds of birds. At the end of May they are getting ready to mate and courtship is in full bloom. Most importantly, the weather is mild compared to winter.

I convinced Sam to let me follow him by promising that I had learned how to be more of a help than a hindrance. He agreed and we started off on one of the strangest journeys I've ever taken.

He began by telling me I wouldn't have to pack much. He had a box already packed with most of our tundra needs – pots, pans, dishes, utensils, salt, pepper, paper towels and napkins. He told me I just needed to bring some apples, vegetables, onions and cup of soups and we'd be fine because he'd be shooting geese for our meals.

We left in the late afternoon. Since it was breakup, everything including the snow on the tundra was mushy and muddy. By waiting till later in the day, the night air would firm things up just a bit for traveling. This made it easier for the skidoo to pull the loaded sled. Since the North Slope has 24 hours of daylight by the end of May, traveling in the darkness was not an issue.

PARALLEL LOGIC

The other good thing about 24-hour light is that the sun can be used for navigation. If you know about what time it is, you can gauge where the sun is in the sky and then navigate from that knowledge in the broad direction you want to take. At least, that's the theory. In reality, you need to pay really close attention to what time it is and how much time might be passing in between checking on the sun's position.

But, I get ahead of myself. The position of the sun was actually not a factor until the return trip and at that point I wasn't talking to Sam anyway. On the trip out, our delay was caused by loss of a river critical to our navigation.

During the journey, Sam admitted to me that he did not, in fact, have poles for the tent. Since I knew enough to know they were fairly critical to setting the tent up, I thought that maybe he should have mentioned this before I left my warm, cozy house with bed. Sam told me not to worry as he'd been given the location of someone hunting near his family's traditional campsite on the Meade River who'd probably have extra ones. It's the probably that bothered me.

His family's campsite is about six hours from Barrow. It took us twice that time to reach its general vicinity due to the little problem of the lost river. We never did find the man with the tent poles. Nor did we find the friends we were scheduled to join up with who did have a tent with poles – Plan B being that we would share their tent for the night and then look for the poles again the next day.

We turned around and went to the village of Atqasuk where Sam's family also had a home. As it turned out, this was good luck for Sam because he was able to catch all the basketball games on TV before we left the next day to continue our search for the poles. It was bad luck for us in general since it was in Atqasuk that he accidentally left all of our knives including his big hunting and skinning knife.

By the time we found the poles, gave up looking for our friends' camp and settled in for the night, it was again rather late. Sam decided to go have a little look round and see what was available for dinner. I headed into the tent to break out the grub box and set up the Coleman stove for a hot meal of fresh goose soup.

We'd set up camp near a pond so we would have fresh water. There were loons on the pond and I found myself humming happily as I set about my tasks. The sound of loons has always had that effect on me. They sound a little crazy and a lot happy – which pretty much defines the state I hope to achieve in my life. We'd finally reached that time on a camping trip I truly enjoy.

Until I opened the grub box. Sam had evidently grabbed the wrong box from his porch. This was the traveling box for short stops to warm up with some tea. It consisted of one broken, metal coffeepot, some tea bags and a can of coffee, about two teaspoons, some white bread and a few paper towels. I guess I should have been grateful I at least had a pot to boil water.

When Sam returned with a goose, his face had that look on it that I was growing uncomfortably familiar with – a look that said "oops!" He'd just realized he'd left his knives behind which was going to make cutting and gutting the goose a little problem. I told him not to worry. With only a coffeepot to cook in, I highly doubted we'd be eating the goose anyway – not unless we wanted to sit there holding one leg at a time in the boiling water.

Ultimately, the two days spent there turned out to be wonderful despite the lack of most common essentials. We ate dried soups and then kept the containers to drink our coffee and tea. We learned to be extremely frugal about our toilet tissue needs. And somehow, as we sat there enjoying the beauty of the late night sun over an Arctic land alive with the sounds and sights of birds, the fact that the only way to stir the tea was with his belt buckle didn't seem to matter.

The journey back home after those two magic days brought me crashing back to reality. The same relatively warm and wonderful weather that had made the two days at camp so special had also melted a lot more snow, and left in its wake a lot of muddy tundra. Muddy tundra has two distinct characteristics – if you have something you need to move over it, it will grip like super glue. Conversely, if you'd like to get some traction for your boots – say you're trying to un-stick a sled that has bogged down in the super glue – you can rest assured the surface will be slicker than some beaches in Prince William Sound.

We battled the mud for hours – though I'm not sure "we" is appropriate. Sam would sit on the skidoo, sled attached, and yell, "Push harder!" I'd lean into the back of the sled while he gunned the engine. We'd move one slow inch at a time until we suddenly hit a firmer patch of ground. Then the skidoo would catch better traction and take off, pulling the sled with it.

I, on the other hand, would be left face flat in the mud. I'd get up and trudge through the mud till I caught up with the skidoo and sled that had – of course – gotten stuck again. Sam would be sitting on the skidoo waiting for me to get into position to push again.

It was in this painstaking manner that we crawled home. Whenever I could catch enough breath to point out what I thought was an unfair division of labor, he'd patiently explain to me that he was the man and so he had to drive the skidoo. He'd also point out that he knew the way. At the rate we were traveling, which could only be calculated in a negative number, I didn't think that mattered.

In the end, our six-hour journey again took over twelve hours. I should mention, however, this was not all due to slow speed. Once we got closer to the coast, the snow really firmed up and we made good time. The only problem was that Sam had miscalculated how long it had taken me to push us this far. He followed the sun thinking it was where it should be for 11 p.m. when it was closer to 4 a.m. Although there is still some debate between us about the real reason for the extra delay – and I am proud to announce that I can now hold that discussion with Sam without threatening him with a sharp knife – the bottom line is that when we hit the coast we were at Peard Bay, a lot closer to the village of Wainwright than to Barrow. It was a miscalculation of some thirty to forty miles. About then I started to think of it as *The Trip That Would Never End* – kind of in the same vein as that song about the man who never returned.

Summer camping is an entirely different experience. We'd travel the rivers by boat then and camp amidst green grass and bushes despite the distinct possibility that we'd lose a battle to some particularly strong battalion of kamikaze mosquitoes. We'd go to Sam's family campsite on the Meade River in late summer trying for the time before the waters froze up but after – hopefully – the worst of the mosquitoes had passed. Since we went by boat, the journey was a little more comfortable and usually a lot warmer.

Rivers in the Arctic can be strange. They have a channel that is deep enough for a shallow shaft motor on a boat to operate without trouble. But they also contain a lot of very shallow spots where the motor can't operate. The idea is to find the channel and not lose it.

We'd put-put along for a little while and then Sam would lose the channel. He'd pull the motor up and grab a rope from the front of the boat that was tied to the bow. He'd climb overboard and wade into the river in his hip boots, sling the rope over his shoulder, and start walking along, pulling the boat and searching for the channel. Whenever this happened, I had to fight an awful impulse to sing "Ol Man River".

If the weeds had the channel too obscured, he would suddenly take a step and start sinking as our first sign that he'd found it. More often than not, however, he'd walk along like this, moving from one side to the other, and eventually see the channel. Then he'd climb back in and start the motor so we could put-put a little further before the whole process was repeated. But it was warm, it was summer and I was doing the sitting this time so I didn't really care how long it took. Which was good cause it usually took quite a while.

Chapter 6

The Arctic Waltz – A Quick Two Step

When I got married in 1975, Barrow was still a pretty quiet little village. The pipeline boom and all its attendant changes were a few years away in Barrow even though Fairbanks and Anchorage were already feeling the pressure.

This meant that the wedding was a very traditional village affair with everyone cooking and baking for days ahead of time to feed the guests at the reception. There were no caterers or restaurants that would host the affair. You found a place like the community center or the church hall to hold it and everything after that depended on you, your family, your friends and anyone else you could rope into helping.

The basic format of the reception was that you went into the church hall after the ceremony. Food was laid out there. While the guests ate, the bride and groom stood at a table in the front of the hall and opened their gifts. With each gift opened, the name of the giver was announced and the gift identified. This was usually done to the accompaniment of much applause and sounds of general approval.

The gift ceremony was a particularly delicate one when you consider that unless the present was handmade, choices had been limited to what the local store had in that month. It's hard to maintain your enthusiasm when you are announcing the receipt of your fifteenth set of napkin ring holders. One of my friends was still giving cookie jars and water glasses away ten years after her wedding. I had enough place mat sets and kitchen utensils to last me till the Second Coming.

I remember the tale that came out of one memorable wedding where the bride and groom joyfully announced the receipt of a six-pack of toilet paper. Always a useful gift and certainly not one of which you are apt to get too many.

The fondest memory I have of my wedding day involves my wedding cake. It was baked and decorated by two wonderful and dear friends who went out of their way to make it the best wedding cake possible. They bought books about wedding cakes; they spent money on the plastic thingies you need for the tiers to sit on; they bought all the plastic squeegees to make the candied flowers; they did everything they could to insure its success.

It would have worked, too, had it not been for one little miscalculation. The way it was explained to me later, they were in the process of making the icing when it happened. The page on the recipe book turned ahead one too many and no one noticed.

The day of the wedding, a group of us climbed into a car, each carrying a stunningly decorated, extremely fragile layer of the cake to be brought to the church hall for final assembly. At the hall, my friends set the plastic stands up and coordinated the placement of one layer atop the other. But the little plastic legs of the stand seemed to be having trouble piercing the icing on the layer below.

Soon, we were pounding rather hard on something that was supposed to be soft and not even getting a dent in the icing. In fact, far from being delicate, the icing had the consistency and strength of cement. Apparently, the page in the cookbook had turned to the recipe for those hard little flowers that usually provide the adornment for the top and sides of the cake.

When we realized that no amount of pounding would pierce the icing, we gently placed one layer atop the other and hoped the little plastic legs didn't slide off before we cut the cake. When the time came to cut the cake, James and I simply turned the knife over and whacked the icing with the handle till it cracked. Then we placed a piece of icing on each plate of cake.

If you think about it for a moment, you can't buy memories as wonderful as that. No caterer in the world could have given me a cake made with such love that even after the marriage ended, the memory of the cake still warms my heart.

PARALLEL LOGIC

Since Alaska is a boom and bust kind of place – for some reason the climate alone is not sufficient to entice people to live here – the state always gets really crowded during these boom times. Of course, that statement is an Alaskan perspective. An Alaskan perspective on the best of days makes parallel logic look eminently sane and reasonable.

During booms such as that produced by the construction of the Alaska pipeline, strange things happen. Your house actually has more value than your outstanding mortgage debt. Hotels are full. Money flows and legislators give whole new depths of meaning to the words "pork barrel". People move into the state lured by the stories of instant wealth. Stories that could be true if they could get out of the state with their pay checks even slightly intact.

But Alaskans have become quite adept at milking the boom times – and those seasonal Alaskans who come here following it.

During the Pipeline Boom, Prudhoe Bay workers often got no further than Fairbanks where an entire culture conspired to separate them from their money. In many cases, the worker was a willing, albeit quite intoxicated, co-conspirator against himself.

During the height of the boom in Fairbanks, people were paying $500/month for the privilege of pitching a tent on someone's lawn. Hookers not only waited at red lights to knock on car windows and solicit business, they went door to door. Sometimes so many would come up to one car it looked like a crowd scene. I know. I was often in the car with my husband when they came up to the window.

We'd be in Fairbanks to do some shopping or visit relatives. Whenever we stopped for a light in town, the car was surrounded. It was as if I didn't exist. The hookers tapped on the window and shouted out various prices and offers. For a graduate of the Chestnut Hill College of Catholic Virgins (they had a hell of an entrance exam), it was an opportunity to learn many things not normally taught in Catholic Virgin colleges.

Soon after our wedding, my husband and I headed east to visit my folks. We had tickets that started in Barrow and didn't stop till we hit Philadelphia. Unfortunately, the only plane into Barrow the day we were leaving was quite late. By the time we arrived in Fairbanks, our connecting flight would be long gone. There was some debate about whether to leave Barrow at all or wait till the next day. We decided if we were at least in Fairbanks, we'd have the best chance of making early connections.

The two things that had not figured into our plans were the Fairbanks airport would completely close down at night and all the hotels rooms would be taken. Welcome to the pipeline boom.

After standing at a telephone using up every dime we had – plus a few loaned to us by cleaning personnel anxious to lock up and leave – we finally found a place that could take us. It was just a little motel on the road leading to the airport.

I suppose I should have gotten suspicious when the desk clerk seemed surprised we planned to stay all night. Or maybe I should have figured it out when he asked if we wanted the hourly rate.

When we got to the room it was, to put it mildly, basic. It was small, there was a cot lined up by either wall, a tin closet at the foot of the bed and a light over each pillow. The only locks on the door didn't work and the bathroom was down the hall. The walls were thinner than paper. Privacy for anything was non-existent.

I spent the entire night sitting up in bed fully dressed, clutching my purse with our honeymoon money in it, while my new husband snored peacefully on the other cot. In between his snores, I listened to the lady in the room next to me negotiating prices. It was quite a learning experience. I didn't even know you could do some of those things, let alone charge for them I felt like I was in the middle of a Robert Service poem titled *They Were The Only Ones Renting The Room For The Night*.

Unfortunately, my marriage didn't last very long. It was over in three short years. James and I split in a mostly amicable fashion and I was able to be happy for him when he remarried and had a family. Over the years we saw each with less frequency than one would expect in a town so small. But when we did we were always able to smile and speak as friends. His new wife and I were even able to form a somewhat more tenuously friendly acquaintance.

But what I found best of all was that the town itself had no problem accepting me again as a single lady trying to survive in the Arctic. His sister and her cousin are still some of my dearest friends – the kind of friends you might not see for months or years but when you do its as though no time has passed at all. I don't know if you can find that anywhere outside of a small town. It certainly has been of enormous value to me during my years in the Arctic.

Many years after my wedding, I found myself stuck at Prudhoe Bay because of fog in Barrow. Rather than spend the evening flying back to Anchorage, I decided to spend the night there and catch a flight to Barrow in the morning. I was brought to a room that was an exact replica of my honeymoon suite in Fairbanks – except the locks worked and I wasn't scared to use the bathroom. I wondered as I went to sleep that night if there was some mad motel decorator loose in America who actually thought tin closets were a pleasant addition to the general motif of a motel room.

About the same time as my marriage, major changes occurred in the way our kids were educated. When I first arrived in Barrow, the BIA ran the school system. Classes only went to eighth grade. After that, you were sent out to a BIA boarding school whether you wanted to or not. Every September, all the teenagers left town. There was little in the way of employment that would have given their parents money for plane tickets. So the kids left in September and returned in June with no visiting and few phone calls in between.

When the North Slope Borough was formed, a School District was also created. The presence of Prudhoe Bay within our boundaries gave us a large property tax base. This meant we could afford the cost of education in the Bush. The BIA was asked to leave town and folks here finally got some say in how and where their children would be educated. Classes were immediately expanded through high school and suddenly our kids were with us all year round. In fact, John Denver was in Barrow shooting a television special when we had our first ever high school graduation and he sang at it.

Along with a high school came sports teams to cheer for – the Barrow Whalers basketball, wrestling, running and volleyball teams played to great cheering crowds. Since there's no competition that's not at least a 500-mile plane ride away, our School District had to get creative to figure out how to have a season. We ended up passing what had to be the largest travel budget for any high school sports department in the United States.

Our away games were scheduled in clusters. The team got on a plane for Fairbanks or Anchorage where they picked up a bus and traveled to the other schools. Enough money was put in the budget to fly an entire team up with coaches and chaperones when it was time for a home coming game.

In the good old days before the onset of the "Bush Yuppie" syndrome, formal wear in most of Alaska meant women wore panty hose under their jeans and men wore the cleanest pair of Carhardts they could find. Since winter is such an omnipresent fact of life here, really dressing up meant a new parki. At times such as Christmas or *Nalukataq*, new parkis with beautiful ruffs and colorful patterns would appear. The women looked like arctic flowers in full bloom. Men appeared in the more formal black or dark blue parki with equally impressive ruffs. The women completed their look with beautiful skin mittens hung on brightly colored, knitted "idiot strings". Idiot strings are knitted loops of rope that go over your head and have your mittens attached to the end. This way, you can shake your mittens off when you enter a house and they just hang down and don't get lost.

They sewed with a variety of materials I'd never seen before. This was probably because my mother was not what anyone would call a sewer. In fact, long after my brother graduated from college, she still had a bag with a half-made sweater she'd started for him when he was about three. Her sewing machine was mostly used to hold plants.

The materials Inupiat women used ranged from wide corduroys to the smoothest of velveteen. Later, denim would also have its day. Some time during 1973, Shontz's store got in multiple bolts of bright Hawaiian print material. Suddenly, women appeared in town looking like tourists who'd lost the bus in Oahu – except, of course, for the fact that the material was topped off with wolf, white and red fox and wolverines ruffs.

When we started having proms, the idea of formal wear was not quite the same as in most places. It's one thing to have a prom or a formal dance when you live in an area where stores that sell the appropriate wear are but a car or bus ride away. Here in the mid-seventies, there was no store like that. Since most people still didn't have jobs, money to buy these items was in short supply anyway.

So the first few proms at our high school involved a wide variety of dress. Some lucky girls actually had new prom dresses. Others wore their mom's best Sunday dress. Oft times, they completed the look with mom's best shoes. Since the weather demanded thick socks anyway, big shoes could be made to fit. Some girls wore clean jeans and a jacket or parki. The parkis, beautifully crafted and hand sewn, were kept on throughout the dance. Old bridesmaid dresses about three sizes too large – usually complemented with mukluks or sneakers – were also common.

The boys had less leeway in their attire but were generally much more relaxed about the whole thing. Basically, they brushed off what they'd been wearing at the gym. Some ordered tuxes up from Anchorage or Fairbanks. Since sizes were a guess at best, these rented outfits often looked as though they'd been ordered for someone else.

But none of that mattered. The whole idea of proms and formal wear was so new that we got to define it as we chose. Since no one could claim to be an authority on a "required" look for the evening, any look you chose was acceptable. It was a wonderfully delightful and egalitarian attitude in which having a good time and feeling good about having a prom here overwhelmed any standards for appropriate dress.

So it was in this fashion that proms first made their appearance here. There was every manner and mode of dress imaginable at the gym. Mukluks, dance slippers and sneakers slid across the floor. Beautiful parkis and the ubiquitous flannel shirt were equally represented. Being selected as king and queen had more to do with being the best liked than the best dressed.

We have gowns, flowers and high-heeled shoes at our proms now. The gym is brand new and the decorations transform it into a fairyland of adolescent dreams and schemes. Just the way it's supposed to be. Yet I still miss the sight of those students dancing across the floor in every outfit imaginable, having a good time because for the first time they could do this at home. It may look more beautiful now, but it was very special back then.

Chapter 7

FelAir – An airline you can trust

It was 1975. I was a newlywed. As such, I wanted to work the day shift so as to spend as much time as possible with my new husband. Although that feeling lasted for an amazingly short period, while it was there it was intense. Since I'd been at the hospital for three years, I was one of two senior nurses. The other nurse didn't want to work a day shift in the outpatient clinic so I figured the job was mine. I figured wrong.

The Director of Nurses decided that somehow, in between my wedding and work, I was having an affair with one of the physicians, the doctor who gave me away at my wedding. This apparently confirmed her suspicions. She decided his recommendation of me for the job as clinic nurse was due to some wild desire on our part to have frequent sex in the exam rooms.

So I didn't get the job. She did tell me I could work the day shift for six months while I broke in the new nurse who was getting the job. I thought about this for a moment. I could train another nurse for the job I wasn't qualified to do. I reserve parallel logic for my own use only. When others try to use it, I am offended by their amateur application of the process. This was a classic example of the power of parallel logic in the hands of a novice.

When she told me she'd hired someone else for the job, I threw my head back, shouted "Ha!" and quit. It was a fine gesture carried out with a grand flourish. There were only two little flaws. My housing was dependent on my job and I was the only one with an income in our family. With one sweeping gesture, I'd become penniless, homeless and jobless. But I'd made my point.

Housing turned out to not be a big problem once I got over any qualms I might have had about calling someone sent to Anchorage for a possible brain tumor to see if he would rent his old house to me. And a job fell into my lap when another nurse, Sonya, told me about an opening at the new municipal health department. She'd started working there after her marriage.

Having never had a municipality here before, the whole concept of "health department" was fairly vague. The North Slope was dominated by the federal government. Villagers had been encouraged to act like dependent children. Suddenly, we not only had the power but thanks to the Prudhoe Bay property tax base, the money to do pretty much whatever we wanted.

I arrived at my first day on the job with the title of "Emergency Medical Services (EMS) Coordinator". This was an awesome title to have in a place with no emergency medical services available. Oh sure, we could try to keep you alive once you got to the hospital, but getting there was a bit of a problem.

The hospital did have a flat bed truck with a couple of canvass stretchers from World War II. If you needed help getting to the hospital, the maintenance man on duty drove over to pick you up. Once you were loaded on, the stretcher was placed on the back seat of the pick up. Everyone then prayed the truck wouldn't go over a big bump and knock the stretcher off the seat. Of course, this beat hell out of the old days when you arrived by dog team or carried in someone's arms.

One of the great memories I have of nursing was when a taxi pulled up to the hospital with a woman in labor. We'd received a call it was coming and that the lady in question was pretty far along. A nurse, doctor and gurney awaited the taxi at the front door. When it arrived, the doors opened and out poured about ten people including a newborn baby.

Apparently the mother had been at a party when labor started. Not wanting to break up a good time, she didn't call a taxi until she was about to deliver. Everyone at the party was concerned about her welfare so they all decided to go to the hospital with her and her husband.

⚜ PARALLEL LOGIC ⚜

The hospital was no more than five minutes away. Of course, in Barrow in 1973, nothing was more than five minutes away. But even five minutes was longer than she could keep her legs crossed. The baby was truly imminent.

As they sped to the hospital, someone noticed Alice Neakok, an aide at the Public Health Nursing Clinic, walking along the side of the road with her young daughter. The cab pulled over and they hauled Alice and Tammy into the front seat. Leaning over from the front to the back seat, surrounded by nine other people and a daughter whose eyes were as big as saucers, Alice delivered the baby.

By the time the cab pulled up at the hospital, everyone inside was celebrating the successful birth. We health professionals were naturally horrified at the unsanitary and dangerous conditions in which the child was born. We hustled both mother and child onto the stretcher and raced to the delivery room. The new mom kept insisting she could walk there but we wouldn't hear of it. A complete and thorough check showed everything looked normal. Yet we knew in our hearts that it was only a matter of time before some fulminating infection would overwhelm both mom and babe. Two days later mother and child left the hospital with no apparent ill effects. It was enough to make us health professionals pretty damn mad.

Having become used to these somewhat primitive pre-hospital conditions, I was unsure exactly what being the EMS Coordinator would entail. Was I expected to coordinate a couple of canvass stretchers and a pick up truck? When I asked around, I found out no one had any clear idea of his or her responsibilities. All five of us – the entire health department – were groping in mutual darkness.

Borough Mayor Eben Hopson Sr. knew most of the staff as PHS nurses since that was our main recruiting pool. He felt if we had aspirin and bandages, he'd be pretty content. And even though it didn't take long for staff to get beyond that concept, for some people, it would always remain our primary role. I soon found myself traveling routinely to Anchorage, Fairbanks and Juneau as one of thirteen EMS Coordinators representing the thirteen EMS service regions in the state.

Except for the one or two people representing urban areas, we all faced similar problems in service delivery and training. We also faced the fact that the State Troopers had been the only agency providing any type of EMT training or pre-hospital services. They were not thrilled at the sight of thirteen hippie-like characters laying claim to their territory.

So it was not unusual, during EMS Coordinator meetings, to have a State Trooper representative show up and place his gun on the table at the beginning of the meeting. This would have been a lot more intimidating had we not been fairly sure it was a felony for him to shoot bureaucrats – even if they were long-haired, dope-smoking, draft-dodging hippies. Not that we all fit into those categories. It's just that most of us fit into enough of them to cause the trooper to be really annoyed much of the time.

The most important part of those meetings was lunch. It got to the point where the printed agenda contained that item as the first order of business. Until we had all decided where and what to eat at noon, issues of cardiac resuscitation didn't seem very important. We may have all been hippies, but we also instinctively knew how to be good bureaucrats.

Somehow, despite the fact that most of us were shooting from the hip when it came to any knowledge of what we were doing, an EMS system for the state gradually took shape. Then all we had to do was convince the Feds to send us the entire gross national product to fund it.

One of the first things you learn when doing Federal grants in Alaska is that no one in Washington, D.C. has the faintest idea of what you're talking about. For instance, most of Alaska is not on a road system. To get there from here, you usually have to fly. So your travel budget calls for a lot of money to be spent on plane travel. Some number cruncher in D.C. inevitably red flags that line item and wants to know why you can't take a bus or train. You quickly find that being a grant writer in Alaska means finding a million ways to say "but in Alaska, it's different . . ." You find yourself explaining the concept of twenty-four hours of darkness and what this does to plane travel to villages with no landing lights.

Inevitably, out of desperation, you invite the key player – i.e. the one who holds the purse strings – to come to Alaska and see for himself. The big problem here, of course, is they all want to come in the summer. Winter holds no appeal.

PARALLEL LOGIC

Which is how I found myself hosting Dr. Dave Boyd, father of all Federal EMS funding, to a trip on the North Slope to find out the realities of pre-hospital care in the Bush. We started off in Barrow and flew to Pt. Lay. At the time, Pt. Lay was a village of about fifty people. It was located on a spit of land that jutted into the ocean and was rapidly being eroded by wind and surf. The North Slope Borough, still in its infancy and wanting very much to do right by its people, decided to relocate the village.

I can only guess that whoever decided on the relocated site chose it in winter when everything was frozen. Because in summer, it was painfully obvious that all the land surrounding the new village site was high and dry. The village, however, sat in about four feet of water. Eventually, the village would be relocated again, this time to dry land. In the Arctic, many houses are built on sleds and are therefore highly mobile. If the first place you plop down doesn't suit you, you hitch your house up and move it down the road. We expanded that concept to include whole villages.

It was in its flooded location when we brought Dr. Boyd there to show him an example of the difficulties of medevacs in Alaska. We flew on an airline called "FelAir". It was named after its owner, Joe Felder. Since I knew the origin of the name, it never struck me as odd. Until Dr. Boyd insisted on having his picture taken under the sign while commenting that he hoped it didn't live up to its billing. The plane was a typical, small Bush plane. It took a couple of hours to get to the village. We had to land at the DEW Line Site because the village had no runway. Then a rollagon took us overland to the river. We were met at the river by a boat that took us across to the village. And then we stood there, knee deep in water, gazing at miles of dry land around us. Dr. Boyd was much too polite – or possibly stunned – to say very much about it.

I wanted to bring him to our health clinic. But the local health aide was at her home in the old village site and didn't want to come across the river. So we sloshed over to the clinic only to find – as I'd suspected – that the door was unlocked and we were free to enter. We entered with about twenty people following in behind us. Apparently a message had gone out on the CB that a doctor and nurse were coming in from Barrow. Villagers were clearly unimpressed with Dr. Boyd's protestations that he was a bureaucrat who hadn't really practiced medicine in quite awhile. All they knew was he was a doctor and doctors just didn't come to Pt. Lay that often. In fact, it had been over a year since the last visit from a PHS physician. So no matter what he said, they weren't leaving till he examined them and their children.

Dr. Boyd spent the afternoon seeing patients and prescribing eardrops and antibiotics. When we left, I'd venture to guess he had a much finer appreciation of the difficulties of pre-hospital care in the Alaskan bush.

Another visitor to our villages was Dr. C. Everett Coop. He came soon after being confirmed as Surgeon General. He came wearing the complete regalia of the Commission Corps including shiny, polished black shoes. He came during breakup.

I hinted that the attire he and his aide wore – while definitely spiffy and classic – was somewhat inappropriate for travel to our villages. Unfortunately, it was too late to send him home for his rubber boots. So we flew to Atqasuk, about thirty miles south east of Barrow. I watched in horror as he stepped from the plane into breakup mud. In retrospect, though, the much funnier part of the trip was watching this staunch anti-smoking advocate get into the cab of a truck with a full load of people who lit up.

Due to some remnant of propriety learned at my alumna, Chestnut Hill College for Catholic Virgins, I chose to ride in the back of the truck so I could light up without feeling rude. I needn't have worried. He'd have never seen me smoking through the dense cloud in the truck's cab.

One really interesting part of being health director in the early days of the department's evolution had to do with the wide variety of tasks that fell upon the director's shoulders. No one else wanted to do them. The phrase "all other duties assigned" soon took on overwhelming meaning in my life.

For instance, take dogs. I'm an absolute, certifiable, completely irrational animal lover. From the time of my first apartment, pets have always been part of my life. Dogs and birds control my home.

But animals have not traditionally held that place in an Inupiat home. Until the advent of reliable skidoos in the sixties, people used dog teams. Dogs were viewed as property. They were working animals in the same way draft horses pulling a plow were. They had a purpose within the scheme of family subsistence and survival and within that context were cared for as you would any valuable possession.

Once skidoos took over, dogs became obsolete. The Inupiat had never viewed them as pets. They'd not considered them something to hug, pet and spoil. When they no longer pulled sleds, they were chained outside to guard the house. They were fed and their areas kept clean. Perhaps out of a sense of overwhelming boredom, the dogs chose to occupy their idle time reproducing indiscriminately.

By the time I got here, the packs of roving dogs had become legendary. They were known to circle the old Wien terminal and pen the tourists up in the summer. There was no vet in town and no care available for animals except what you could convince one of the docs at the hospital to do. The acceptable method of handling the dog pack problem was to shoot them.

There was an animal research facility down the road at NARL but the staff members were research scientists. Even they brought their animals to the hospital when something went wrong. Which is how I got to see my first wolf up close and personal.

He was brought in on a stretcher to the hospital emergency room in the evening after regular clinic hours. The wolf had been the subject of some experiment on why a wolf's paw doesn't freeze in sub-zero temperatures. We treated the wolf for frostbite on his paw. Science had apparently just proven a wolf's paw could freeze.

Our lab tech also got to go to the polar bear cage at NARL and draw blood on the resident bear. It certainly helped break up the humdrum routine of human medical care.

In between treating wild animals, we also saw domestic pets at the cargo door of the hospital. When someone needed his or her dog tranquilized before a plane trip, we'd take a guess at the dog's weight, call a vet for an appropriate dosage and then try to figure out how much people medicine equaled that much animal medicine.

We also did some spays in the patient exam rooms after hours. Well, actually, we did one spay on the dog of one of the docs. He did it figuring it couldn't be much more difficult than doing it on a human. The surgery took about as long as triple by-pass surgery takes today. It turns out it was a lot different than doing it on a human – especially when the dog seemed to be losing a lot more blood than necessary. And it wasn't as though we had some kind of canine blood bank available.

Hell, we didn't even have a human blood bank available. We'd joke about having a "walking blood bank". This meant that in case of emergency, the lab tech got on the phone with her index card of people in town with the right blood type and asked them to come to the hospital and donate blood. It made emergencies just that much more exciting when you got to run around looking for people to give blood at 3 a.m. while trying to stabilize a hemorrhaging patient.

Sometime in the mid-seventies, a decision was made to close the animal research facility (ARF) at NARL. A vet was brought on board to oversee the placement of the various animals still there. The polar bear got to go play stud at a zoo in the Northeast. The vet, Dr. Les Dalton, smelled as though he should have been left with the bear after he finished riding in cargo for over 24 hours with his tranquilized patient.

Eventually, he had so few animals left at the facility that he found himself getting bored. As a new health director still groping for direction on needed programs to develop, I was all ears when Les stopped by my office and volunteered his services. Because he was a military vet, he was cross-trained in environmental health. We had no sanitarians providing regular inspection of food serving establishments, so it sounded like a good two-for-one deal.

The only hitch was that he would need an assistant. And that ugly little phrase "all other duties assigned" reared its head again. Since uncontrolled reproduction among now idle dogs was a major cause of problems, spaying and neutering animals became a priority. So did shooting all loose dogs because of the wide spread rabies problem. Between the two methods, we felt there was some hope for cutting the problem down to manageable size.

And in his spare time, Les could inspect the meat counter at our local store and confirm if the shiny green colors really were just packaging problems.

When the spaying and neutering program was confined to Barrow, it wasn't too hard on me to assist. I'd just have to get up a little earlier – say 5:30 a.m. – in order to get out to NARL by six for the first surgeries. We'd spay dogs till nine and then I'd clean up and go to my office.

But when we moved the program out to the villages, I got a real taste of frontier medicine gone nuts. Les and I would go to a village that rarely saw a human doctor and try to convince people to let an animal doctor care for their dogs. We'd explain the dangers of rabies, the horrors of dog bites. We'd literally go door to door in sub-zero temperatures begging people to let us spay or neuter their animals and give them immunizations.

Finally, Les hit on the idea of getting through to the kids. We'd make pitches in school and send them home to lobby their parents. And just to sweeten the pot, we told them they could come and watch as we performed surgery on their pet. It was that promise that finally turned the tide. In a small village in the late seventies with no TV or movie theater, watching your dog being spayed sounded awfully good and bloody. Bloody was very important to kids being deprived of their requisite dose of murder and mayhem Hollywood style.

We were in the village of Kaktovik when the first real breakthrough occurred. A boy came up after class and said his family said it was OK to operate on their dog. Unfortunately, the clinic being used by the health aide for human patients was an old Quonset hut with a faulty heater. It spewed black dust over everything when it turned on. This was obviously not ideal for surgery. It wasn't ideal for humans either, but if you worked hard, you could get into the rhythm of the blower and see patients in between cycles.

We got permission to use the old community center for our surgeries so long as we finished and cleaned up before bingo. Bingo is very important in Bush Alaska. If you interfere with it, you risk any and all good will you may have previously generated.

We set a table up in the middle of the hall under the one good light we could find. It wasn't the best light but was as bright as we could get. When the boy arrived with his dog, he also brought along about twenty friends – just about every kid in the village under sixteen and over eight.

Les was thrilled. He figured they'd all be so impressed they'd go get their dogs too. And he was probably right except for one small glitch that occurred twixt thought and action.

The surgery began in a fairly propitious manner. The dog went under easily. The incision went smoothly. In fact, I was almost relaxing. I had the portable suction unit ready in case Les needed some fluid removed to clear the incision area. The kids were all bent over the table as far as we would let them short of sticking their faces in the dog's open abdomen. And then I heard it. One small word that would change everything.

"Oops!"

It was a quiet cry but one that caught my immediate attention since it was quickly followed by a spurt of blood. Then another spurt. Then I heard the kids muttering. They were saying things like, "Wow!", "Lookit!", "All right!", and the ever-popular "Cool, man!" Les, whom I respected then and respect now as one of the best vets I've ever had the privilege to work with, had accidentally snipped a small artery. Under normal conditions, this would have been no problem. Under normal conditions, an assistant would have redirected a strong operating room light into the abdominal cavity and the bleeder would have been located and clamped in no time flat.

What we had was a fluorescent light in the ceiling and the flashlight I was holding. As the blood spurted and the kids responded ecstatically to what they thought was normal and extremely cool, Les groped frantically in the dog's abdomen clamping off just about anything he could find. As each clamp went on, we would hold our breath for a second. Inevitably, the blood would spurt again.

As we worked frantically to stop the bleeder, both of us were acutely aware of the fact that if we blew this surgery and the dog died, our entire program of animal control would be blown out of the water. To say nothing of the fact that we both preferred to not have the dog die on us while his loving master and multitudinous little friends were watching.

After what seemed like an eternity, we finally clamped off the bleeder and finished the surgery in record time. We carried the dog home and explained that he might sleep a lot over the next few days due to the anesthesia. We went back to the Community Center and frantically cleaned up all the blood before the Bingo players arrived. Then we went to our lodgings and prayed as hard as we could that the dog would live.

Our lodgings were with a bush pilot named Walt and his lady friend who had two cats they wanted spayed. While she made dinner, Les sat at the kitchen table and operated on the cats. We all sat around and drank coffee and watched. When dinner was ready, we put the cats on their pillow, wiped the table and ate.

In the end, it took the dog about three days to wake up from the surgery. We checked on her every few hours the first day. We tried to pretend this was normal for an "older" dog that had surgery. The family was gracious to us though they clearly were a bit startled at just how long it took before Fido wanted to get up and play again.

I'll always be grateful to that dog for not dying. She held the credibility and future of the vet program in her paws. And she did the right thing.

Les eventually left the military when NARL closed and came into town to develop our Vet/Public Health program. It was a combination that took some time to fine tune but ended up working better than I'd ever imagined. Not only did we now have a humane way of handling animal problems short of running around town with a shotgun, but we also had someone routinely inspecting eateries to assure that they changed their frying oil at least once a month.

Because Les was well aware that I was a pushover for anything within the animal kingdom, I found myself being pulled into various adventures with him when least expected. For instance, there was the time I had a snowy owl living first in my living room and then in my qannitchaq while he healed from a wing injury. You have no idea what an odor really is till you've had a sick snowy owl laying his droppings in the confines of your house.

The Inupiat name for Barrow is *Utkeagvik*. Loosely translated, it means "place of the snowy owl". The tundra around Barrow abounds with snowy owls. It's a major nesting area for these birds. Their population rises and falls in conjunction with that of the lemming population since lemmings are a major food source for the owl.

Some kids had found this particular snowy owl while exploring on the tundra outside of town. Someone had shot at it and damaged one of its wings. The kids brought it into the vet's. The bird was near death with awful smelling gangrene in the wound under its wing.

Les, his assistant Cyd, and one of the deputy directors at the health department, Sarah, worked hard to clean up the wound and stem the infection. (Yes, Les now had a real assistant. I'd learned enough about being a bureaucrat to hire someone else to get up at 5 a.m. to spay animals with him!) Then he attempted to place a small straight pin in the bone of the affected wing to strengthen it enough to allow the bird to fly again. This was critical. If the owl couldn't fly, he'd never return to the wild.

Once the surgery was completed, the problem arose of where the owl could recuperate. The vet clinic was a small house in the middle of town. Snowy owls are very big birds. Some accommodation would have to be found. And once again, that ugly little phrase "all other duties assigned" reared its head in my life.

I was living in a Borough house that had a relatively big *qannitchaq* (that's an Arctic cold storage porch). What better place for the owl to live? A dear man named George Leavitt donated his huge dog carrying case as a cage for the owl. Since the case was large enough for his St. Bernard, we felt it could hold the owl, which was promptly named "George". George (the human) went so far as to cut holes in the sides of his dog case to place a perch so the owl wouldn't be in close contact with his droppings.

This cage was hauled over to my house and the bird, still too sick to protest, was formally ensconced in my living room. At that time, my buddy Sam was in between relationships and inhabited the couch in my living room. I thought the owl would make a good companion for him while he looked for a human one. He didn't see the humor in the situation – especially when the odor took over. However, George (the human) was Sam's big brother so he couldn't complain too much about living with George's namesake.

Lovey, on the other hand, took one sniff and vacated the living room for my bedroom from whence she did not emerge until all this foolishness had been worked out of my system. I think she viewed this as just another example of my failing mental health. As for my birds (I had acquired another parrot, Captain, by then), they were absolutely insulted that I thought bigger might be better and retreated to the far end of their cage to alternately sulk and screech.

George (the owl) was eventually moved to the *qannitchaq*. I fed him from a spoon with his medicine wrapped up in the food. When the neighborhood kids found out what was going on, they started to appear with all kinds of meat scraps for George. When he got better, he made it clear he preferred the scraps to the canned dog food. The kids vied to bring in bigger and better scraps for him. I started to worry that they were actually bringing over daddy's caribou steak dinner.

As George got better, he also got feistier. When he first arrived, I actually spent some quality time with him when feeding him and giving him his medicine. When he got better, my hand stood in imminent danger of being snapped off every time I tried to get medicine or food into him. I eventually suggested to Les that perhaps the time had come to see how well George really was.

This was a critical moment. If his wing had not healed enough to carry him in flight, we were faced with finding a home for a handicapped snowy owl. Sam had made it clear that even if he wasn't paying rent for living on my couch, he still had some rights and one of those was the right to not share his space with a loud, smelly, feathery companion. Or, at least, not to have to share his living space with more than two loud, smelly, feathery companions since Adeline and Captain had laid claim to the living room before he had.

For some reason, my incurable optimism had me envisioning a "born free" kind of experience in sending George back to the wild. We would toss him skyward and he would slowly circle as he got his bearings, dip a wing in salute to those who saved him and then take off into the trackless wilderness to live out his allotted time span as God and nature intended. I have a rich fantasy life.

In actual fact, the scene looked more like a Keystone Cop comedy. With every kid in town following us, Les carried George to the playground across from my house. It was a big open field with lots of room for George to use to get airborne. We removed the chain from his leg and Les tossed him skyward amidst cheers and applause.

George plummeted back to earth with astonishing swiftness. We had barely reached the refrain "as free as the wind blows" when he hit earth. The wing had not healed even slightly. It was clear George's flying days were ended.

We cleared the kids away with promises that they'd be kept apprised of George's future plans as soon as we had some. In the end, George was lucky. We found a zoo that wanted him for his reproductive capabilities. While he may not ever know the freedom of the wind beneath his wings again, spending his life as a stud in a zoo can't be all bad when you consider his alternatives.

We had another George in our lives a few years later. He was a walrus pup found trying to suckle on a ship's rope. The ship, part of the Canadian fleet, was in Barrow for a few days while on its regular summer cruise schedule. The sailors waited to see if a mom was around. When it was clear the pup was on his own, they pulled him in and brought him to the vet's clinic.

The vets contacted the appropriate federal agency since walruses are protected under the Marine Mammal Protection Act. Eventually, the path was cleared to send the pup to the new Sea World in San Antonio, Texas, after a brief detour at a marine mammal center that made sure he was healthy enough to survive.

Once again, though, we had the problem of what to do with a walrus pup while waiting for the paper work to clear and the plane arrangements to be made. Since Sea World pays all expenses in cases like this, we didn't have much involvement other than keeping the pup happy and fed until we were told what to do. We also needed to keep the pup as isolated as possible since too much human contact would have placed a lot of stress on him.

As always, George Leavitt, who has a heart as big as Marlon Brando, came to our rescue and said we could place the pup in his garage until arrangements were completed. In keeping with the tradition started with George, the snowy owl, the walrus pup was named George after his benefactor.

I had occasion to visit the San Antonio Sea World a few years later. George was happily housed as one of the star attractions. And my old buddy Les was the chief vet. I got a four-star tour of the facility that included a private visit with George. It's one thing to view a full-grown walrus from a distance while he responds to commands in a show. It's another thing altogether to find yourself in his quarters, up close and personal.

Upon command, George came over and gave me a kiss. Not only did his breath smell as though he were belching a thousand dead fishes, but walruses have this saliva akin to that of a St. Bernard. It's wet, slimy and distinctly unattractive. And no one warned me about it before he planted a kiss on my cheek. On the other hand, it wasn't half as bad as some dates I've had.

Chapter 8

You Lost A What?!!!

When I first came to Barrow, I thought all planes were big and had jets engines, flight attendants and stale peanuts. Any other planes that existed had no bearing on my life so I pretty much ignored them. I'd never been in a plane until I was twenty-one and making my first journey to Europe. What I learned then was that I didn't particularly care for the entire relationship.

Don't get me wrong. I'm not one of those "If God meant man to fly he'd have given him wings" crazies. I am perfectly willing to admit that flying is often the best way to get from here to there. After all, I moved to a place usually accessible only by air. I wouldn't have done that if I didn't accept that airplanes have their place in the scheme of things. It's just that I view them the way I view flossing – a necessary, but not necessarily pleasant, fact of life.

During my whole six-hour orientation to nursing in small Alaskan villages, no one ever mentioned medevacs. Had they, I might have had serious second thoughts about the wisdom of an Arctic adventure.

When I first arrived in Barrow, medevacs were handled by any aircraft in the vicinity that could be pressed into service. Everything from hercs to jets full of tourists served our emergency needs. As did very, very tiny little planes that God clearly never really meant should be up in the air without a safety net.

My first medevac from Barrow was done on a herc. I had a patient in a coma on a stretcher hooked up to a respirator, which consisted of an oxygen tank with a gauge contraption welded to the top. The oxygen tank was of the huge green variety that was never really intended to be portable. On the other hand, the can-do spirit of the Bush asserted that if you put wheels on it, just about anything is portable.

The herc had come to Barrow full. It was unable to off load because the one piece of equipment capable of unloading it was broken. It was returning with the same full load. This meant there was no room in its enormous belly for a patient, a stretcher, an oxygen tank and me. So we went up to the cockpit.

For those of you not familiar with how big a herc really is, let me just say you have to climb stairs to get up to the bottom of its belly. That's one level. Then you get inside and you climb another flight of stairs to get to the cockpit.

Since the cockpit already had a full crew complement, the addition of me, my patient and our attendant paraphernalia was more than it could hold. The stretcher was shoved up the stairs. I followed. The oxygen tank was left downstairs. A very long piece of tubing connected my patient to his oxygen. The stretcher stuck out into the opening of the stairwell leaving a very tight space for maneuvering. In order for me to check the oxygen level, I had to hang upside down from the cockpit, peer down the stairs, and shine my flashlight on the gauge.

Once we were airborne, the captain explained to me that he once lived in a remote section of Alaska with his wife and children. His daughter had taken ill and he'd gotten on the radio to send out a frantic message for any plane in the area to come and help him get his daughter to a hospital. A nearby plane picked up the message, changed its original flight plans and went to his rescue. He said that ever since then, he always went out of his way to help when people needed emergency flights. I have never heard anyone in all my twenty-eight years in this state better express the spirit of Alaska.

The Alaskan night was clear. The stars seemed but a few feet away. I had my barf bag nearby. It seemed as though I could relax. And I would have were it not for the sudden movement that started on the part of the crew. One minute they're laid back and chatting, the next minute they're hitting switches, flipping pages in some thick manual, tapping gauges with their fingers as if not quite believing what they'd just read. And I knew I was going to die without ever meeting Little Joe.

After what seemed like an eternity, but was actually about 60 seconds, one of the crew turned to me and suggested I put my seat belt back on. Needless to say I had not only never taken it off, but I had it cinched so tightly I still wear its imprint on my shoulder. I asked him what the problem seemed to be. If I was going to die, I was curious as to the cause. Well, he explained, it seems we lost an engine.

My first reaction was intense anger. What did he mean, they'd lost an engine. How could you lose a very large engine? Why wasn't someone outside looking for it? And wasn't this just the height of carelessness – misplacing an engine in the middle of a flight. Highly irresponsible, I'd say.

Before I made a complete idiot of myself, the other possible meaning for the term "lost engine" came to mind. Then I really panicked. I looked over at my patient, who was critically dependent on his oxygen supply and wondered how I would be able to parachute out and keep all three together – patient, tank and me.

Luckily, the crewmembers sensed my concern. The fact that I had withdrawn into a fetal position while whimpering may have clued them in. One came over to comfort me and assured me we would still make it to Fairbanks, it would just take a little longer. And that is how I've viewed flying in the Bush ever since – we'll get there, it just always seems to take a little longer.

Another experience that will stay with me forever was the day I took a critically ill patient out on a plane full of tourists. They put the stretcher in the front and the seats started right where the stretcher ended. This would have been bad enough were it not for the fact that the patient had a very communicable disease. He was unconscious through the trip and when he did stir at all he was combative. Because of this, we had him strapped to the stretcher.

He was a strong young Inupiat male who was completely out of it due to meningoccocal meningitis. When he came to and tried to sit up, he'd strain every muscle in his body and I would watch the straps stretching till I was sure they would break. What I would have done at that point is beyond me since I had this horrible vision of him running up and down the plane totally out of control with me following behind trying to shoot him up with Valium.

Of course, the tourists on the plane had no idea that he had such a communicable disease. So every one of them decided they had to go to the bathroom during the hour and ten minute flight to Fairbanks and every one of them chose to use the front lavatory which just happened to bring them past the stretcher. I wondered if they would have been so anxious to get a first hand view of the action if they had known the diagnosis.

I liked it better when they just put the stretcher and me in the cargo area where we had some privacy. Take offs and landings were fun. The stretcher would be strapped to the rollers. We would be surrounded by packed igloos. I got to sit on the rollers and cling to the stretcher. I kept my mind occupied wondering if the flight attendants would remember to notify me if the plane was in trouble. I tried to remember if, like the captain and his ship, the nurse had to go down with her patient.

After the North Slope Borough developed a Search and Rescue Department, medevacs became a lot tamer and easier. The Borough actually invested in planes designed to carry emergency medical equipment and personnel. I found I honestly missed the challenge of taking a patient out on a jet full of tourists and trying to keep him alive till the first stop.

The planes that fly in the Alaskan Bush between small villages are – of necessity – small. This means they have no bathrooms. Every time I knew I would be taking a flight on one of these delights, I'd stop all fluid intakes about three days prior to departure. It wreaked havoc on my kidneys and bladder but was the only way to be assured that I would not find myself choosing between a pain worse than death or trying to discretely pee in a coffee can. I also stopped all food intakes so that when I got airsick I wouldn't have much to offer to the god of nausea.

I must admit that most Bush pilots attempted to be somewhat sensitive to these miseries if only because of the enforced closeness of a small plane. And I made some incredibly valiant efforts to not barf until after the plane had landed.

To this day, the smell of pickled herring can cause a wave of nausea in me most people can't even begin to imagine. This is because of an unfortunate moment I had once on a small plane when the passenger seated behind me passed an open package of it around for anyone who wanted to munch. As the package passed under my nose, reverse peristaltic action in my digestive system caused an immediate, uncontrollable urge. Needless to say, no one passed food around when I was on a small plane with them after that.

One good thing about the intimacy of Bush communities is that word spreads quickly. One incredibly brave pilot actually put me in the co-pilot seat next to him on the theory that the ride was smoother up there. Maybe it was. I couldn't tell because we picked up a passenger who had obviously just awakened from some major party. He reeked of the night before the morning after. I held on as long as I could and then unfortunately caused a small mess on the instrument panel. After that, I was seated far in the rear of the plane with a very large plastic bag.

Bush pilots tend to be breeds unto themselves. Most sane people give them wide berth. I found over the years that the wisest way to handle them was to be very accommodating. For instance, there was the time we were landing at Kaktovik. Our pilot – who for reasons soon to be obvious will remain anonymous – really wanted to land. He didn't plan to let anything interfere with this decision – including a rather thick cloud cover.

We circled what I assumed was the general vicinity of the landing field for a few minutes while our pilot carefully scanned where the ground would have been had we been able to see anything at all. I assumed we would soon be turning back to Prudhoe Bay and I checked my watch to see if we'd get there in time to catch a late flight back to Barrow.

Even as I was looking at my watch, I felt the plane's nose go down into what seemed like a straight dive. I thought for sure we had run out of fuel or the engine had died and now we were all going to crash. But no, our pilot actually seemed to be voluntarily doing this to us. We broke through the clouds about ten feet above the runway. He straightened the plane quickly and we touched down about a second later.

My friend Jim was on this trip with me. He was in the back seat. As we taxied on the runway, I heard him say – in a rather shaky voice – "I thought you had to have at least one hundred feet of clearance before you could land." Our pilot shot him a quick look and said, "Oh, we had at least that much." Jim – who is about 6 foot 3 inches tall – got out of the plane. I couldn't see his head through the fog. Yep, looked like a hundred feet to me.

I finally took to eating vast quantities of Dramamine before getting on one of these flights. This had the added advantage of putting me to sleep. I decided I no longer cared if I was coherent when I landed so long as I didn't humiliate myself during the flight. However, even this plan had its moments. Like the time I was snoozing peacefully and felt the motion of the plane change. As anyone with a fear of flying knows, any change in the movement or sound of the plane while in flight is indicative of immediate death due to the plane falling out of the sky.

I came instantly alert and looked out the window to see my last sight of earth before going to meet my maker. Instead of the sky or earth, I found myself looking into someone's camp tent. It seems that our pilot wanted to buzz his family's fish camp to say hi. So he flew in low and sideways – certainly one of my favorite positions while in an airplane.

One time, my medicine wore off before the flight ended due to the fact that we were being held in a circling pattern while waiting for one of the big jets to land. Our pilot decided to fly out over the ocean ice and describe circles with the plane – circles which became smaller and tighter with each pass as he tried to see how tight he could get them. I don't know how green my face got but I do know that when he happened to glance up and see it he paled and immediately straightened the plane up. We landed very soon after that.

One of the nicer things the North Slope Borough has done here – at least from my perspective – is to purchase helicopters for the Search and Rescue Department. For reasons I will probably never understand, I can be hanging sidewise and upside down in a helicopter while it is buffeted by high winds and not feel the slightest distress whatsoever. Given a chance to ride on one, I am willing to accept just about any extra job or task.

I knew I was over the hill on them the day I actually enjoyed flying out in a blizzard on one. We needed to bring someone to the village of Atqasuk to be their health aide since their regular one was sick. It was the weekend and they needed some sort of emergency coverage. Due to the blizzard, I requested assistance from Search and Rescue to get the alternate health aide out there.

In reality, there was only the slightest of justifications for me going along on the trip. Actually, I'm not sure "keeping the pilot company on the return" even qualifies under slightest. But I didn't care. I went along. The wind howled and the snow blew and I sat in that helicopter like a baby in its mother's womb.

Planes are not the only scary modes of transportation in the Bush. One of my earliest contacts with the realities of taxis in the Bush was the day an old man was brought into the hospital soon after I came to Barrow. A taxi had backed up over him. Then the taxi reversed itself and drove back over him a second time. We undressed him with trepidation, fearful of the damage we'd uncover. What he had were tire tracks that went across his chest in one direction and came back across his abdomen in the other.

You see, it was breakup and the mud was thick and soft. The taxi had merely squished the old gent down into it. He had some bruised ribs and a very sore belly but was otherwise OK. As for the taxi driver, he apparently drove off completely unaware of any thud that might have occurred.

There were few if any garages in the old days in Barrow. Spare parts were expensive and hard to obtain. Taxis were kept running on sheer guts alone. They were dispatched through the most primitive of systems – in some cases the driver went back to the owner's house and picked up all the calls that came in while he'd been on his last run.

In order to accommodate as many passengers as possible, the taxis would pick up as many people as could possibly fit and compressed five or six separate calls into one marathon response. Taxis are a lot more regulated in Barrow now than twenty years ago. You are no longer apt to find yourself squeezed into a cab with ten people who are on the third day of a party that you didn't attend.

My favorite Barrow cab story involves a good friend named Michael who had gone out to NARL to pick up a couple of fares going to the airport. As he drove down the road to the airport, he noticed a tire roll by him on the driver's side that was going at a fairly fast clip. It occurred to him that since the cab was the only car in sight, perhaps there was some connection – or, in view of its independent journey, should have been.

He was right. In actual fact, his left rear tire seemed destined to reach the airport before the paying customers. The taxi was apparently staying upright through sheer momentum.

As he came to a safe if ungainly stop, he turned to his passengers in the back seat to explain there would be a slight delay while he reconnected the tire to the cab. He told me later he took one look at their faces and thought, "Now I know why they call you white people."

Skidoos are a ubiquitous part of life in Bush Alaska that also qualify as questionable transportation. Although their function as motorized dog teams is certainly unquestioned, some other recreational uses can be fairly scary. I once spent a very interesting afternoon on a sled being pulled by a skidoo through a riverbed. Because the skidoo is actually traveling on ice and not snow, speeds can be increased.

My husband and I were out for an afternoon drive with his brother Abel and Abel's girlfriend, Sherie. Both James and Abel had skidoos pulling sleds on a long rope. The only weight on the sleds was Sherie and me respectively. This meant the sleds could move easily over the ice. It also meant that each time the skidoo swerved even the slightest, Sherie and I got to play "whip-the-lash". The sleds would skid madly towards each other while traveling at a high rate of speed. Just about the time I could count all the fillings in Sherie's teeth – her mouth being opened in one permanently frozen scream by then – the guys would manage to get enough traction to pull them apart.

Pushing the limits of just what skidoos can do is a popular sport among young people here – especially the men. Skidoo racing is one form this activity takes. But my favorite is cliff climbing. Since we don't have any mountains nearby, the cliffs on the beach are used for this activity. The skidooer will go out on the ocean ice a distance and then head the skidoo back towards land and the cliffs. He guns the motor and picks up speed as he approaches them.

He has two basic options for activity on the cliffs. One is to race the skidoo up the side of the cliff as fast as possible, then take a sharp downward turn and end up back on the beach – preferably still attached to the skidoo and right side up. The other option is to continue racing up the cliff until your machine's nose bursts above it. Then, the theory goes, gravity and motion combine to bring you crashing down atop the cliff. Once again, proper form requires that you and the skidoo are still attached and right side up.

One of the most wonderful people Barrow has produced this century is a man everyone around this state knows simply as "Big Bob". Bob Aiken is one of those gentle bears who comes along once in a lifetime with a commitment to leave the world a little better for having been here. He is a force to be reckoned with in every sense of the word. Only there is one force that even Big Bob can't overcome. That is the force and law of gravity.

Perhaps my most favorite piece of super 8 film is a scene of a group of skidooers on the beach near Barrow back when we were all a little younger and a lot more flexible. The men were engaged in racing skidoos up the cliff. Each tried to go a little faster than the last so that when they broke through at the top, they would go higher in the air before the front nosed down and they crashed back to earth.

The film showed one skidoo after the other breaking through at the top and leaping into the air like a land torpedo gone mad. And then came Big Bob. Big Bob, as one might surmise, got his nickname from being the biggest guy in town. He carried a little more weight up the cliff than the others. The film shows him starting up the cliff at a fairly fast pace. But the skidoo starts to slow down long before the top of the cliff is in sight. Gravity and motion are clearly doing battle and gravity is winning.

With much effort, Big Bob kept the skidoo going forward until he reached the bottom lip of the cliff's top. But there was no energy left in the skidoo.

Unlike the little engine that thought it could, Big Bob's skidoo just simply couldn't. With barely a perceptible sigh, Bob got off the skidoo, lifted it over the top of the cliff, then turned to the camera and waved a victory sign. Now there is a man with class.

My personal favorite in the "fun to ride" category is the three-wheeled Honda. Unfortunately, they have been banned from production due to the amount of accidents they engendered. Four-wheelers are now produced, but without the fear and danger factor, they seem kind of dull and lifeless.

Riding the original three-wheeled Hondas was like learning to ride a horse. You had to get to know your particular machine personally and hope you got one with a nice disposition. Having a nice disposition meant it wouldn't crap out on you five miles out on the tundra because you misjudged the depth of the river you just crossed. Having a nice disposition meant it would start on the first five or ten pulls and not make you pull the starter rope until your eyes bled.

Having a nice disposition also meant it wouldn't rear up and throw you like a bucking bronco while you tried to figure out the intricacies of its gear shifting. I spent a good deal of my time on the ground dodging a three-wheeler about to overturn itself on me by rearing up as I attempted to find first gear.

The other thing I quickly learned about these monsters is that three wheels simply do not turn as quickly as two wheels. Nor do they turn as sharply. Well, actually, they do. It's just that sharp turns cause the outside wheel to rear up and long before the turn is complete, the rider finds him or herself dodging a spinning machine.

Once I mastered driving a three-wheeler – which included compromising on certain issues like sharp turns – I took off to explore the tundra with my two dogs. Lion, son of Lovey, was an active healthy male who loved to run. Lovey, as has been mentioned previously, did not have quite the same attitude towards physical exertion. She felt that motorized vehicles had a motor for a purpose and saw no use in trying to run beside one.

I'd take off across the tundra with Lion loping along beside me only to turn back and find Lovey following at what could only be called a sullen distance. Inevitably I'd end up trying to balance her on my lap on the front of the Honda as I bumped along on the tundra. She sported a look that indicated the twenty feet I'd made her run had exhausted all her reserves of strength.

But perhaps the most interesting transportation of all in the Arctic is by dog team. While I am well aware there are experts in this field who can hitch up a team and take it for a run with no more effort than you or I might put into starting the car and taking a Sunday drive, my experience with dog teams occurred with a friend who didn't quite have that level of skill.

Sherie, who shared wild sled rides with me, was also my sister-inlaw for a brief period. Her husband Abel had a dog team. He was working towards a shot at the *Iditarod* – known to anyone who has been in Alaska over three hours as the "last great race".

When Abel was not around, Sherie took responsibility for the care and feeding of the animals. This sometimes included the need to exercise them. Sled dogs like to run. They are trained athletes. If they haven't gotten their regular exercise for a day or so, they tend to be very excited when they finally get hitched up. Sled dogs are also fairly strong. Controlling them, especially when they're excited because they're about to get a run, takes not only strength but the ability to bark orders in a loud, forceful baritone that will get their attention. Sherie had that down pat.

But when Abel wasn't around, she needed some help with the run. For reasons I will never understand, she thought I was qualified to be her assistant. Considering my spectacular lack of success in ever getting Lovey to obey any given command – or even to acknowledge that she heard it – I can only wonder at what she thought my qualifications were.

One of the first times she asked for my assistance was in February and about as cold as it gets here. If I remember rightly, it was about twenty-five below without wind-chill. I had a temporary roommate named Hank who happened to be a strapping young man. Since he worked for me – as did his aunt – I felt no compunction whatsoever about dragging him along on the adventure. In fact, he was actually excited about getting to work with a dog team.

We managed to get the team hitched up with Sherie yelling only a little – and hardly at all at the dog team. She wouldn't have had to yell at me either had I been able to hear through the layers of scarves, ruffs and hats I had pulled up around my ears.

Once the team was hitched up, I sat on the sled to give it some weight. Sherie would mush from behind. Hank got on the sled with me for the ride. I was almost ready to enjoy myself as much as I could, given the temperature, when I heard Sherie shout the command for "go". And go they did. At least the front half of the team. Somehow they had not been tightly connected to the back half. So we watched the first six dogs take off across tundra in fine form and with great speed.

Unfortunately, the four dogs left behind tethered to the sled could not move quite as fast because of their load. In fact, they really didn't move at all. They mostly barked madly and got very excited at the sight of their teammates having a good romp without them.

I don't think I ever fully appreciated just how low Sherie could get her voice to register until that moment. She certainly got my attention. Unfortunately, it wasn't my attention she wanted. And the dogs were clearly having a wonderful run with no intention of slowing down or stopping in the near future.

Sherie and Hank took off on foot to chase the dogs. My job was to remain with the sled and the four dogs still attached to it. It was, thank God, a job I am capable of doing even in temperatures of twenty-five below. They were gone for what seemed like most of my life. A job that had started out easy had now become life threatening. I was in imminent danger of freezing to death because I had nothing to do but sit with the dogs.

When Sherie and Hank finally returned, I received no sympathy for my complaints about how stoically I had faced death rather than desert my post. In fact, they were so far from sympathetic, they sounded down right snarly. Seemed the boys on the team had smelled a female in an interesting state and had pursued the smell despite all obstacles. By the time the chase was completed and the dogs recaptured, they had had quite an adventure.

Upon breaking loose from the sled, they had immediately headed towards town where they could definitely scent a femme fatale. The most direct route there involved going through people's yards. Some of these people had dogs in their yards. Some of those dogs objected to the passage of six crazed dogs, tethered together and of one mind and purpose. To put it bluntly, Sherie and Hank had not had a pleasant time.

But, having already been through so much effort, it seemed a sin not to run the dogs and give Hank his first experience with a dog team. Hank agreed and we took off for a fairly good run.

We were out with the team for at least an hour or two on top of the time we had spent chasing them. By the time we got back to the house, even old Arctic hands like me were pretty chilled. Hank walked somewhat gingerly to the couch and started to take off his boots very carefully. I wondered what was wrong, as I'd not seen him hurt his legs or feet in any way.

As he pulled his boots off, my eyes widened in disbelief. There was a large tear in each boot that left the inside sock completely exposed. He was wearing sorrels and inside each sorrel was a mouton sock. Except the mouton socks were completely worn through around the heels. So he had basically just spent about three hours in snow and ice with temperatures of twenty-five degrees below zero with less protection on his feet than you would normally wear for a tropical rainstorm. Needless to say, his heels were absolutely white from frostbite. So were some of his toes. I shuddered to think of the pain he was about to endure when his feet thawed. Luckily, he had no idea of what he was facing.

I guess I'd forgotten how incredibly macho men need to feel when they're in their early twenties. When I asked Hank how he could have done something so incredibly stupid – a question both Sherie and I asked in very calm and polite tones – his response was that he wanted to help with the dog team and figured he'd be OK. Only twenty-one thinks he can walk barefoot in snow and ice for three hours and not have it be a problem. Only twenty-one can carry parallel logic to those heights and actually convince himself it might be true.

Hank ended up in the hospital. When this was first suggested, he pooh-poohed the idea that he would need that level of care. Why, he'd just take two aspirins for the pain and tough it out. We didn't argue with him. We let the pain of his feet thawing out do our work for us. In the end, he was pretty lucky. He stayed in the hospital a few days with his feet up and on pain medication. But he didn't lose any part of his feet. As they say, God protects fools and children. You can put him in whichever category you'd like.

There was one other time Sherie got me to run the dogs with her that is particularly memorable. It was during the muddy season – which, in Barrow, is anytime it's not frozen. Since there's no snow cover for the dogs to pull a sled, Sherie and Abel had acquired a purple glitter dune buggy from a dump. They stripped it down to four wheels, two seats and that lovely purple frame. They also claimed to have kept some version of a brake though I still think that's a subject open to debate. They would hitch the dogs to this eye-catching little number and take off for a run.

One of the few drawbacks to this was that without windshields, the people driving the team tended to get spattered with mud. Now remember, this is Barrow where mud is being studied by scientists as a possible new life form. It is mean, ugly and deadly accurate when splashing on you. It hardens to cement-like consistency within seconds after hitting its target. Minutes after a run started, the driver and passenger were indistinguishable blacks blobs periodically heard to cry out "gee", "haw" and "Oh shit! It got in my mouth!"

This was the condition Sherie and I were in when we hit the beach at NARL. We dripped black from head to toe. The only part of our hair not wind blown was the part too packed down with mud to blow around. Because we were aware this would be our condition, we had started out the run with grungy clothes. Now we resembled badly washed bag ladies.

As the dune buggy moved along the beach at NARL, we saw that a barge was unloading down the beach and we wouldn't be able to mush straight through. Since the dogs were not yet tired from running, they were still somewhat excitable. While Sherie is a wonderful woman in every way possible, the reality is I never really believed she had full control over the dogs – especially if they made their minds up that something else was really interesting.

I think Sherie knew this also. So the decision was made to turn up off the beach before we got to the barge and start a long circle back towards town. Only the dogs wanted to gee when she said haw and wanted to haw when she said gee. A good deal of time and distance was expended before Sherie and the dogs got their terms synchronized and we actually turned up from the beach. Unfortunately, we turned up right at the spot where there was a large mud puddle. A very large mud puddle. A very large mud puddle that the dogs plunged straight into before realizing they were not going to be able to actually pull the dune buggy through it.

When they ran out of options (these options apparently consisted of pulling straight ahead until we were absolutely stuck fast), they decided to take a breather and see what ideas their musher might have.

Well, truth be told, Sherie was a little angry by then. And though you wouldn't know it from her sweet and ladylike exterior, she does have a fairly extensive scatological vocabulary that she can use when needed. I know this because I heard every word in that

⇘ PARALLEL LOGIC ⇗

vocabulary, strung together and spoken in one breath, in the five seconds it took her to get out of the dune buggy and realize just how deep the mud was and just how stuck we were.

Much to our chagrin, we were not the only ones aware of the situation. By the time we had turned off the beach, we'd reached the barge. By the time we got stuck, we were but a short distance up from it. As we turned, we saw ourselves being closely watched by the roustabouts off loading it. Some of them were downright cute.

Unfortunately, that was not a statement any of them would probably have made about either of us. From their observation post, they saw two possibly female, definitely mud-covered, figures stuck in the middle of a swamp. One of these figures was letting loose with an extremely creative stream of questionable language while hauling dogs around by their harness. The other figure was now standing behind the dune buggy trying to push and starting to imitate the first one's vocabulary.

This is possibly the first time in my life that my physical presence, combined with my vocal utterances, stunned a group of young studs into silence. Unfortunately, it was not quite as I ever imagined it would be. I'd always hoped it would happen in a dimly lit bar and my figure and dazzling conversation would silence the room and bring every man there to his knees. Instead, I was up to my knees in mud and sweat and their silence had more to do with fear and awe than adoration.

A few of them took tentative steps towards the sled. Whether they were doing this because of some imagined obligation to try and help or to get a closer look at the creatures creating the disturbance is something we will never know. We saw them approaching and were hit with a superhuman power that enabled us to move that dune buggy out of the mud and on down the road in record time. I think the power came from the awful thought that they might get close enough to actually identify us.

A few weeks later, Sherie traveled to Kaktovik on a business trip. Kaktovik is the last stop on the eastern end of the barge's route. Since there were few accommodations available, she ended up eating at the same bunkhouse as the barge workers. She was panicked that one of them would recognize her as the lady from the purple dune buggy. No one did. But she did manage to overhear a conversation going on at the table behind her in which one of the roustabouts amused his table mates with the tale of a purple car pulled by dogs that got stuck in a mud puddle while they unloaded in Barrow. An inordinate amount of the tale was given over to a description of the two women who were driving it. It was not flattering.

He'll never know how lucky he was that her embarrassment over being one of those women outweighed her anger when she heard his description.

PARALLEL LOGIC

Chapter 9

The Tyrannosaurus Rex Mosquito and other Arctic Summer Phenomena

As the years went by, I grew to understand that things are just different in the Arctic. We did things differently and we thought about them differently. For instance, just about anywhere else in the world they have four seasons – four seasons that are fairly recognizable by any standard. Here in the Arctic we also have four seasons – they are the dark season, breakup, the light season, and the "I-can't-believe-it's-already-snowing" season.

It's probably a toss up as to which is worst – the dark cold of winter or the sucking mud of breakup. Breakup is that lovely time of the year when all things turn to mush – specifically, the ground beneath your feet. You step down onto what had once been solid footing for your journey through life. Instead, you find the high tops of your breakup boots disappearing accompanied by the soft sucking sounds made by a sentient creature seeking sustenance. You instantly know that if you don't pull your foot out quickly, the mud will turn ugly and devour it. As you slowly regain control of your foot and boot, you hear a hollow pop. This is the sound of the angry god of muck and mire. He is letting you know that while you may have won the battle, the war has just begun.

I've watched many friends – some of them strong women who have survived long, dark, cold Arctic winters with multiple toddlers underfoot – finally break down sobbing as those same toddlers come in from playing during breakup. Just getting them to take off their shoes on the porch doesn't help. This mud has its own consciousness and knows that trick. That's why it's secretly hidden itself in every fold and crease of their socks and pants. They drag this primordial ooze throughout the house – ooze that harbors life forms as yet unknown to the human race. I'm told that if you're very quiet, late at night when all the lights are out, you can actually hear these life forms giggling and conspiring as they reproduce. You can even see the tiny tails of smoke from their cigarettes when they're finished.

My most vivid memory of breakup concerns the standing pools of water created as the snow melts. Permafrost starts about ten to twelve inches beneath the tundra. It's permanently frozen soil that can't absorb water. This means the land gets waterlogged very quickly during breakup. Melting snow that can't be absorbed in the soil ends up sitting on the top of the ground while slowly draining towards the sea. Sometimes it just sits there till it's absorbed in the air. However you look at it, there's a period of time when a lot of water hangs around in places that don't normally have swimming pools blocking access.

By the time this particular breakup occurred, I'd left nursing and was director of our new municipal health department. I'd just recruited a dentist and his wife to start a dental program. Jim and Janis are very nice people who came here from Coronado, California – a place where breakup refers to relationships and not seasons. Because they were so nice, they didn't ask too many questions when they awoke one morning to find their entire house surrounded by about three feet of water. It seems they'd moved into new municipal housing that had been built in a depression. The surrounding roads were at least a couple of feet higher than the ground on which the house stood. When breakup happened, not only did the snow in their yard melt and create a standing pool but also all the snow from the surrounding areas drained into their depression.

Since I lived nearby, I would stop on the side of the road near their house to give them a ride to work each morning. I watched, as they emerged in hip boots suitable for deep sea wading. They carried their shoes, briefcases – and occasionally their boxer Sam if he'd not yet been carried to dry ground to relieve himself – high over their heads. If the current wasn't too strong and the fish weren't biting, they usually made it to the car in about five minutes. You have to pick your way very carefully through a sea created by breakup gunk. You never know which life forms might be gaining dominance down there.

When they reached the car, they'd take off the hip waders and replace them with our normal waterproof, knee high, black rubber breakup boots. In the lower '48, spring means the advent of white and pastel colors in shoes. In the Arctic, it's a signal for black.

Each year as I watch the mud building up under my tires in the garage, or I look at the muddy, wet dish rag wagging its tail on my porch – the tail being the only recognizable part of the dog I had chained out only a moment ago – I remember Jim and Janis slogging bravely through that water and know if they could survive so could I.

Winter here is a little longer and a little colder than most people like. It starts about August and ends about June. The temperatures actually don't drop below zero until sometime in November. Since the sun will set for the last time at the end of November, you find yourself distracted from the cold as you prepare for your last glimpse of it for two months.

By January, it's really chilly. The normal temperature is about twenty below though there can be many days of really cold weather in the fifty-to-seventy below range. Add in the wind-chill factor and winters can be viewed by some less hardy souls as harsh.

I personally like the winter weather. It's only occasionally, and then with usually good provocation, that I find myself questioning the validity of the winters in my adopted home *vis a vis* its viability as a human habitat. For instance, there was the time we had a flu epidemic here in the dead of winter. Half the town was down and out. The flu travels quickly in the Arctic winter because everyone is pretty much confined inside.

Opening the windows for fresh air is frowned upon. So you breathe and breathe again air that has made everyone sick to begin with. Sometimes, if you're really lucky, you get the same flu twice – once at the beginning of the epidemic and then again as it's making its final end run.

I had the flu. Of that there was no doubt. By the time this flu hit me, Lovey had been dead for a year and replaced with a vet clinic reject named Mr. T. Mr. T felt he should be allowed outside at a minimum of once every twelve hours. In this he greatly differed from Lovey who would hold it for twenty-four hours if the alternative were going out in really cold and stormy weather.

So there I was one morning, looking as lovely as ever in fourteen layers of clothes, shivering in the warmth of my house, thinking death could be possibly easier than living with the flu, when Mr. T decided that no matter how close to death I actually was, I should put him out one last time. I opened the door to a standing cold of forty-eight degrees below zero. With wind-chill, it dropped to eighty below. You haven't really experienced all life has to offer until you've opened a door on eighty below weather while already shivering from the chills of the flu. I don't know what's more ludicrous – living in a place where the temperature drops to one-hundred-ten below with wind-chill or living in a place where the weather bureau calls off the wind-chill advisory because the temperature has gotten up to seventy below.

I think it all really hit me when I came in from putting the dog on the chain and went to the freezer to get something out for dinner. I realized my hands felt warmer in the freezer than they had in gloves outside. When your hands are warmer in your freezer than outside your front door, you remember that moment with startling clarity. Its like the day that you first figure out that your mom and dad did "it". You're never quite the same afterwards. As I crawled back into bed, hacking and coughing and feeling about as sorry for myself as possible, I vowed to never again spend a day where the temperatures outside routinely got colder than my freezer.

This is a vow I often make in the cold and dark of winter. As the snow piles up on my driveway and I find myself climbing up and out of my front door, I try to remember why I thought this was a good idea in the first place. Then, just when I think I've flashed on a solid reason to explain my commitment to the Arctic – and I do not use the word "commitment" lightly here – another blast of cold air tears through my coat and rips the thought right out of my mind.

Yet, just when I think that parallel logic has worked its magic on my psyche again, the temperatures rise to only ten below and the sun comes back for its first tentative peak over the horizon in two months. The world around me reappears white and new and as big as the universe itself.

When the sun goes down, the darkness closes everything down around you. Changes in the landscape and on the sea ice occur in darkness and often in relative silence except for the constant rush of the wind. When the sun does come back, it's like a flower unfolding. The world of the Arctic opens up with the return of the sun. And when it finally reappears, you discover a whole new landscape.

The flatness of the tundra has been carved by the wind and snow so that it's never the same one year to the next. The pack ice creates jagged sculptures along the pressure ridges – a moonscape in ice. The sky seems bigger and bluer than ever before. And I fall in love all over again. I wonder how I could have ever dreamed of leaving this world of sweeping whiteness, icy blues and chilled seas. I never want to lose the feeling of awe and reverence inspired by a land so clean and brilliant in the sunlight that you'd swear the earth had only just been created. I just wish we could settle on something less than fifty degrees below zero as the price of that beauty.

Inevitably, when the memory of winter's cold and darkness combines with spring breakup to erase even those thoughts of beauty from my mind, summer comes, the tundra dries out and the world here explodes with life and beauty. And mosquitoes. In fact, the Tyrannosaurus Rex species of mosquito is found only on the Alaska tundra. It is slow, lazy and lethal. That's possibly why, when the summer comes and we actually have days that stay consistently above freezing, my disposition is apt to get worse instead of better. It's because I'm being held prisoner in my own home by that malignant spawn of hell called the Arctic mosquito.

In fact, if I'm not very careful, I'm apt to find myself looking out the window as another gorgeous day of fifty-to-sixty degree (above zero) weather begins and thinking, "Oh shit, it's going to be another nice day". A nice day tends to give our mosquitoes even grander ideas of their size, strength and numbers. Give them a few days of above sixty weather and these close kin to hell's own king get the kind of megalomaniacal ideas that have toppled governments in the name of divine right.

I remember heading out on the tundra one day to enjoy the beauty it has to offer. I was tastefully attired in my trusty Jungle Jim hat with long net. To set it off, I had selected a lovely army green mesh jacket that had spent the entire previous night soaking in mosquito napalm. One drop from this jacket could pollute a river the size of the Mississippi for a year. I was ready.

And so was the tundra. When the weather is hot and the mosquitoes are flying, so are the birds. It's their version of a movable feast. They fly and swoop and glide through the air and seem to be enjoying the effort. The snowy owls sit by the side of the road glaring with imperial disdain as their less serious brethren take flight in the sheer exuberance of life. Where just a few days ago the tundra was still brown and bare looking, the sunshine has caused an eruption of green shades interspersed with tiny, colorful flowers. Like the original inhabitants of the Arctic, the flowers are sturdy but shy and built close to the ground so as to better survive the constant Arctic wind. Anyone who has ever admired the art of bonsai would find the tundra a place of endlessly fascinating and breathtaking beauty done up as Mother Earth's very own bonsai garden.

Of course, all this would have been much more enjoyable had there not been dozens of mosquitoes clinging to the veil over my face laughing their horrible laugh that says, "You can run but you can't hide". I knew without a doubt that despite all precautions, I'd get home and find that somehow, somewhere, they had indeed struck.

That night when I got home, I stripped slowly and inspected every inch of my body for their tell tale signs. Sure enough, there they were – five of them on my left anklebone alone. Somehow, despite thick white socks that had been sprayed with bug juice and covered by long pants with elastic ankles, they'd managed to find their way. Five days later I was still using Benadryl to stop the itch.

The nice days of summer are usually so limited that you really don't have time to do much more than the outside chores you have been putting off since the snows first fell last year. For instance, want to wash your car? Be prepared to run outside and do it fast on the one day where it's warm enough for the glass cleaner not to freeze or thicken before you wipe it off. Want to wash your windows? Find a similar type of day but one with no wind so your house doesn't freeze while you attempt to wipe off a year's worth of muck, grime and dust.

Thinking of a barbecue? Here's a challenge. Find a day where the breeze will not cause the flames to burn your house down. The day needs to be warm enough that the freshly barbecued food does not freeze on its way into the house. But it shouldn't be so warm that you have to fight Tyrannosaurus Mosquito for what scraps of meat he might leave on the bone. There is nothing quite as sad as watching a chef try to protect his freshly grilled salmon with his body as he makes a mad dash to the house followed by the mosquitoes that ate Milwaukee.

No, I didn't move to the northernmost city in the United States for warmth and sunshine. If I had wanted warm, I would have flown straight on when I hit Seattle instead of turning right. Of all the seasons of the Arctic, winter is indeed the best. We know how to do snow and blizzards here like nowhere else in the world. In the end, I guess every one has to be good at something.

Elise Sereni Patkotak

Chapter 10

Gas Toilets: The flames that burn the brightest!

I guess now is as good a time as any to bring up the subject of honeybuckets. I've alluded to them in previous chapters but never really gone into detail. So here it is, ready or not. Everything you never wanted to know about alternative toilet systems available wherever fine buckets and plastic bags are sold. I'd suggest that if you're snacking while reading this book, now is the time to start that diet.

Having been brought up to believe that flushing toilets and flowing water from a tap were part of the same birthright that gave me TV on at least three channels, I found the adjustments to alternative toilets interesting. Honeybuckets were the primary system when I first came here but there were other less popular and infinitely more complicated systems tried in the search for the least odoriferous options. My two favorites were the gas-fired jets and the salad eating throne.

Gas-fired jet toilets actually functioned as a viable alternative for quite awhile at NARL. Their biggest drawback was the smell put out through the vent. The minute you started to get up, gas jets flared on to burn everything you were leaving behind. The force of those streams of fire shot more than one guest out of a bathroom before they were completely redressed. When you think your precious parts are about to be fried, modesty doesn't matter.

The odor of burning material wafted in whatever direction the wind blew it. If you had a neighbor in that direction, they not only knew how often you went, they soon learned to discern what you did while there. If your urges occurred during their meal times, you were considered a less than desirable neighbor.

The salad throne, known conventionally as the humus toilet, was less odoriferous but demanded to be fed a very specific mix of vegetables. If you did not feed it on demand and as needed, it stopped working. Then you had a real problem. You see, the theory on this toilet was that ultimately we are all placed here to create fertilizer for others to use. The humus toilet spent its life making fertilizer in your bathroom out of whatever materials you left behind. It sat up about two steps from the ground to create enough space for the fertilizer being created.

Each year a maintenance man would come to your house and clean it out. He'd add new starter and you were set for the year. For the system to continue to function, it needed a certain balance of nutrients over and above what the family might place there. So, you gave it lettuce, carrots and celery and wondered if feeding your toilet a balanced meal really gave meaning to life. I guess this just proves that the honeybucket is truly the safest, cheapest, least hungry and most fool-proof alternative available.

Here's the way they work. You get a bucket, place a plastic bag in it (optional if you're willing to clean it a lot more than I was), add some blue chemicals beads or pine-scented cleaner, a little water as a starter, and put a toilet seat and lid on top. You now have the standard, Bush issue, never gets clogged, toilet. Once you've experienced this beast, you'll understand why I say the odor of pine will always carry a very distinct message to my brain that has nothing to do with sunshine and fresh air.

Of all the items of Bush life that caused raised eyebrows and snickers of disbelief when I first described it to my family, honeybuckets were clearly the hands down winner for biggest collective shudder. As my mother once put it, "Your ancestors moved to America to better themselves, to be able to flush a toilet... you have just negated a century of struggle."

I never meant to do that to my grandparents. In fact, I struggled mightily to keep from ever getting up close and personal with them. But one day soon after my marriage, I found myself moving from hospital quarters to town housing and there it was – my very own version of hell. In fact, having a honeybucket as a newlywed provides some interesting depth to the phrase "for better or for worse". Getting one's other half to empty the trash is child's play compared to the discussions that can follow a request to empty the honeybucket. You've never really known true happiness till you've thrown a party in which a full honeybucket is carried through your living room because the beer has caught up with your guests and it has to be emptied for round two.

Many, many years later, a friend told me a story about honeybuckets at her dinner party. By the late 80s, the North Slope Borough had gone a long way in providing affordable housing with flush toilets. My friend lived in an apartment in one such unit.

I'll never forget the look on her face as she described the night she had people to dinner and there was a knock on her door. She answered the door to find two gentlemen from the municipality's housing maintenance division. They requested permission to use her bathroom. Since she was aware they were working on a nearby apartment's toilet, she assumed they needed to answer nature's call and graciously invited them in. They promptly reached behind themselves, picked up two honeybuckets full of someone else's overflow, walked through her living room past her guests, and emptied the buckets in her toilet. Since her bathroom was right off the dining area, everyone was close enough to hear all the sound effects.

Words can't possibly describe what this will do to the smartest of dinner parties. It does, however, leave you with enough leftovers to make it through an entire week of lunches.

There are those crazed aficionados of the honeybucket who champion its virtues with a certain air of desperation. "After all," they'll reason with you, "it never gets clogged or bursts a pipe when you need it." I personally find that attitude a bit much even though I still have a honeybucket stashed away in my garage for emergencies. I will admit they are better than nothing – and certainly better than finding a dark spot around the back of the house in 40 below weather. But if you have a roommate – or just plain mate – this lovely object can make or break the relationship in ways you can barely imagine.

For instance, if your mate of the moment feels that filling it to the brim without spilling a drop is a personal challenge, you've got major problems. This is apt to be brought home with brute force if you're the first one up in the morning. You try to use it only to find all available space occupied.

Until the Borough started to provide regular honeybucket pick up service, negotiations over emptying it made nuclear arms reduction treaties look easy to achieve. Then spring would come and you'd get into that ever-popular battle over taking the winter's accumulation to the dump.

The ultimate thrill comes when it's time to clean these lovely objets d'Bush. If your marriage, relationship, friendship, etc., can survive the moment when one of you has to get close enough to actually scrub it out, your relationship can survive anything.

When I was a newlywed here in Barrow, running water was simply not available. You either chopped and melted ice for cooking and cleaning needs or you had it delivered by one of the new water delivery services in town.

This meant that when it came to washing clothes, you had very few alternatives. For instance, you could work hard to maintain friendships with people who worked at the hospital or school. A social event such as a dinner or card game would be planned and you'd show up with your laundry bag and detergent. What host could refuse you? Or it became a barter arrangement. We'll keep you supplied in caribou and fish if you let us use the washer in your laundry room.

If these options were not available, you bought a ringer washer or a side-by-side, very small (as in two jean capacity) washing machine. Since I was apt to lose my fingers to the wringer washer type, I opted for the side-by-side variety.

When the waterman came to fill up your water barrel, he would fill up the washer and tin tub next to it at the same time. The tin tub contained your rinse water. You started with your cleaner clothes – mostly your whites – and ran them through a wash cycle but did not let the water drain out. This was especially important to remember when you consider that the drain hose was not hooked up to anything. It just trailed out behind the machine.

When the wash cycle was completed, you lifted the clothes by hand to the wringer side. You took the hose that came out of the back of the wringer side and held it over the washer side while the clothes spun. This put the soapy water back into the washer for you. You lifted the clothes again and placed them in the big tin tub of water. You rinsed by hand till you were relatively sure the soap was at least slightly rinsed out and put them back in the wringer. You held the wringer hose over the tin tub of rinse water so the relatively soap-free water being spun out of your clothes went back into the tub. You repeated this procedure for all your loads, working from cleanest to dirtiest. You never changed the water unless you absolutely had to because it had gotten so gross even your husband was commenting. It was a system that gave new significance to the simple phrase "Laundromat".

Along with varied alternatives to running water and flush toilets, I also had to get used to the idea that food did not necessarily come all cut up, cleaned and prepackaged. That, in fact, some things like meat might actually show up in my kitchen looking like the animal they once were. Since I was intelligent enough to realize it didn't make sense to eat hamburgers but balk at eating caribou because I'd seen it with its clothes on, I made an honest attempt to adjust. As with all my best intentions, this one was often challenged by reality.

For instance, there was the first time I was requested to make caribou head soup for Easter. This is actually quite a tasty dish. However, making it involves getting very personal with a caribou's head and all its attendant parts. Telling myself that my grandparents used to make goat's head cheese didn't help half as much as it should have. Eyeballs in my soup are just never going to be a comfortable moment for me.

And eyeballs were not the only parts of an animal I'd have to get used to finding when I sat down to eat. The Inupiat are subsistence hunters who use all parts of the animals they kill if at all possible. This means when you have duck or goose soup, you'll find the feet of said animals included in the broth – as well as their heads. Despite this often being the tastiest part of the soup, if you were not brought up looking at soup that looked back at you, it made for a strange experience.

Cleaning these animals preparatory to making a meal can also be a unique experience for someone who thought pork chops were born with little socks on them. Actually, that's not entirely true. I grew up over my dad's grocery store. He was a butcher. I'm well aware that pork chops actually had their socks put on by my dad. The point is, however they got there, they were there before I had to have contact with them. In Barrow, my hunter of the moment was not apt to have even gutted the goose. After all, he shot it. Now its was my turn to do some work.

And do it I would. I'd strip it, dismember it, clean it, make sure to save and clean the gizzard, heart and other delectable innards for inclusion in the soup, and end up with feathers and spattered blood from one end of the house to the other – to say nothing of the condition of my clothes, hands and face. But it would be done, even if my house looked like a set from "Friday, the 13th."

Another habit fairly ingrained here is that of leaving the caribou in just a few large-sized pieces to be cut up later as needed. They're left frozen outside in a protected area. Some parts are hung up to dry and later soaked in seal oil. I liked it that way since preparation was minimal.

If you wanted to make a roast, though, you needed to remember to get it cut up and inside at least one day before the planned meal. Otherwise, you found yourself attempting to rip it apart while it was still frozen hard at forty below. Since most caribou seem to have acquired half the gravel of the North Slope in their butts, the cook is required to spend a good deal of time making the roast safe for human consumption from a dental point of view. If you're attempting to clean up a duck or goose, there'll inevitably be buck shot scattered tastefully about its various parts that poses the same threat to dental health. And if you're working with a piece of meat you forgot to thaw first, you can be assured of chilblains on your hands before you finish.

That's just the way it is here. And what with the price of fresh stuff in the Arctic, becoming a vegetarian is not a viable alternative – though it's one often dreamed in that cold moment when a solidly frozen caribou butt is staring at you from your sink.

Chapter 11

Your Holiday Operator Loves You

Holidays in Barrow are familiar yet different. We celebrate the Fourth of July along with the rest of the country but we do it under the midnight sun. This means we have to save our fireworks until New Year's Eve or they'll be a little hard to appreciate. It's not easy for man-made light to compete with the brilliance of the midnight sun traveling along the ocean like some giant chariot wheel run amok.

A few years after I arrived in Barrow, the traditional Fourth of July parade was born here. Local legend holds that one day the fire trucks were being moved from one side of town to another. Some National Guard members saw them moving in line and thought it must be a parade. So they ran to the front and marched along. One thing led to another and soon a parade was born.

Although the parades have grown bigger over the years, they're still the one thing in town that's not been co-opted by progress. The parade draws its main flavor from the fact that every emergency vehicle in town is in it. The vehicles are usually carrying at least a thousand madly grinning children whose parents are running alongside trying to get their picture. Candy is being flung off the vehicles by firefighters dressed in space suits.

Every flat bed truck available is called into service as a float. Some are elaborate, creating whole tableaus in paper-maché. Some have more tissue paper flowers attached than roses in the Rose Bowl Parade.

All the water and sanitation trucks in town also get in line and you have yourself one credible parade. There may not be any marching bands but the sirens and horns create their own cacophony. We did once have a band ride and play during our Spring Festival Parade. They admitted the cold took some getting used to when it came to blowing the horns. Since they didn't volunteer to come back and do it again the next year, I can only assume they were still trying to grow skin on their lips.

I should explain that the Spring Festival – *Piuraagiaqta* in Inupiat – is our way of marking the transition from the bitter cold of winter (when all outdoor activity is at a minimum), to the bitter cold of spring (when all outdoor activity should be at a minimum but we just have too much to do).

The worst of winter is past and skin boats for whaling have been brought down from their racks to be refurbished and supplied with a new skin cover. Skidoos are being torn apart and rebuilt and sleds are being repaired. This is one last weekend of community fun before the hard work of replenishing the ice cellars and getting fresh meat for the table begins in earnest. Most importantly, the weather is regularly zero – perfect festival weather.

You may not think you can enjoy standing around in zero degree weather eating hot dogs and Eskimo donuts while watching people play golf on a frozen lagoon using green balls. You'd be wrong. It's some of the best fun in the world. My personal favorite is the contest where you have to pull a sled to a set destination, unload and set up the stove, make tea, then pack up and get back to the finish line first. The Olympics have nothing that can even compare unless you've taped the bobsled competitions and are watching in fast forward.

My other personal favorite is the one dog sled pull. This consists of some poor family dog whose tail is wagging furiously because he obviously wants to do his best for god and family. If only he had a clue – a clue as to why he is tethered in this strange contraption while people all around him are yelling and cheering; a clue as to why his usual play pal is sitting on the sled behind him looking like he or she is waiting for something to happen. Could that something involve him?

It's enough to get a poor dog confused. Cause him to go the wrong way. Or have a little bathroom mishap. Or maybe just decide to lie down and wait till all the excitement passes and his family starts to act normal again.

Inevitably, one of the dogs figures things out – or just accidentally heads in the right direction while chasing the smell of boiling hot dogs – and a winner is declared. It may not be the Fur Rondy but it's all ours.

Perhaps one of the best holidays I've ever spent here was the day the circus came to town. Statistics alone don't tell the story but they're pretty impressive. 35,000 pounds of equipment, an elephant, a lion, a cougar, llamas, bears and ponies, 28 performers and an entire big top tent flown up here on one herc from Fairbanks. When it ended, 4000 people attended three performances including 200 children flown in from Wainwright, Kaktovik, Anaktuvuk Pass and Pt. Lay.

The year was 1976, the day was July 5th, and the event was Barrow's officially registered Bicentennial Event. The DeWayne Brothers Circus had come to town. Perhaps the most startling sight was an elephant in the Arctic – an event that had not occurred since the hairy mammoth roamed the tundra hundreds of thousands of years ago. The elephant's name was Bimbo. When her handlers set her up for pictures, old and young alike gathered for miles around to sit on her and be snapped for posterity.

Tremendous excitement was generated whenever Bimbo answered nature's call. When an elephant does it, it seems so large it just commands your attention. It was large enough to cause many of us to stand in a circle around the elephant pointing and exclaiming in awe and wonder at what Bimbo had just deposited. Some members of the Pt. Barrow Lion's Club thought it appropriate to shovel about fifteen pounds of Bimbo deposits in a plastic bag and store it in the Wien Airline's freezer. They thought they'd be able to auction it off at some future date to clear up any left over circus debts. Unfortunately, when they went back to reclaim their manure, it had disappeared. No one would admit to having the faintest idea of what happened to it. At least, that's the story put out by the Lions. For those of us who were regular Wien passengers – and since it was the only airline in town at the time that included just about everybody – this is the kind of news best heard over ten years later.

The circus had been the brainchild of the Pt. Barrow Lion's Club with some help from the clubs in Fairbanks and College. Some of these dreamers – the same ones who'd later think that saving elephant manure for an auction was a good idea – had obviously gotten a bigger case of cabin fever than normal during the preceding winter.

Stories from that day abound. Restaurateur Fran Tate remembers that the herc had to turn back during its initial attempt to come to Barrow because the elephant moved during the flight. They had to return to Fairbanks to secure her. This happened after it had taken them almost three hours to get her to board the plane in the first place. A recalcitrant elephant is a very immobile object.

When the plane finally landed and Bimbo emerged, the excitement was too much for some Lions to handle. So in typical boyish fashion, they expressed their excitement by dumping a fellow Lion, Jimmy Nayakik, on her back. Jimmy says his clearest memory of that moment was just how far it was to the ground.

Once Jimmy was safely rescued from her back, Bimbo was given a walking tour of town. She seemed to approve of everything she saw until she got to the ocean. I guess it's hard for an elephant from the tropics to understand that even though something looks solid it is, in fact, ocean. So she unknowingly put her dainty little foot on the ice and promptly crashed through it. And just as promptly removed it with a trumpet of disapproval. Cold feet were not to her liking and ice chips between her toes were a big turn off.

Aside from Bimbo, there were ponies to ride, llamas to gaze at and over 5,200 bags of popcorn to be devoured during the three performances. The Lions sold over 1700 adult tickets even though those under 18 and over 65 were admitted free. Most of the community spent the day at the circus watching every performance they could get a ticket for and having their picture snapped at every possible place; with the llamas, next to the tent, besides the roustabouts as they drove the tent stakes into the permafrost, and – of course – next to any large deposit made by Bimbo.

Two other traditional holidays that are celebrated quite differently here are Thanksgiving and Christmas. Both holidays are celebrated as village feasts. The two main churches in town, Presbyterian and Assembly of God, host the largest of these feasts.

Congregation members cook up vast quantities of traditional foods from caribou soup to *quaq* (frozen, raw meat or fish that is usually eaten dipped in seal oil).

Everyone goes to church to eat in the afternoon. Everyone, that is, except for those of us with relatives elsewhere. We're not able to make it to the feasts because we're on the phone listening to the latest computerized telephone voice saying, "I'm sorry, all circuits are busy now. Will you please hang up and try your call again later."

When you spend an inordinate amount of your holiday time hitting the redial button on your phone, you have lots of time to think. You find yourself wondering how late you'll be to your holiday dinner party. You hope your hosts understand that you can't leave your house for any festivities until this call has been completed.

Why? Well, because it's impossible to enjoy the good cheer and fellowship of a holiday meal knowing that somewhere back east your mother is sitting at the family table talking about you in the past tense. She'll be saying things that sound suspiciously like a eulogy. She'll ask your sister what part of your inheritance she'd like when the will gets changed. If you're lucky, you get your call through just before your cousin, the lawyer, is formally asked to make the needed adjustments to the document.

Once you do get through, though, your problems are not necessarily over. You'll find that the only line out of state available on holidays is the "echo line". In a typical conversation on the echo line, all speech passes over the wire at the same time no matter how long either party waits to speak. Conversation usually consists of phrases like, "What did you say?"; "No, you go first. I'll wait."; "You're starring in a nude musical?!"; "Oh, you're starting the food now." Finally, someone gives up and shouts "Have a wonderful holiday!" and passes the phone on to the next relative. And thus begins Part II of "Holiday Phone Conversations from Hell".

Not only do you have to figure out which relative you're speaking to based on a two or three second sound bite, but you also get to try and send a meaningful message to them across the miles in the few seconds available before they pass the phone to the next relative. Then you begin the process all over again. Occasionally you do engage in actual conversation. When that happens, it inevitably revolves around exactly what time it is in Alaska, how cold it is there and how nuts you have to be to live there. It's about then that I take to reminding them that the acorn does not fall far from the tree so they should be careful about statements made concerning my mental and emotional stability.

I'm convinced I could live in Barrow for a thousand years and most of my family – a group that is normally functional and intelligent – would never figure out the time change. And Uncle Joe will always ask for the wind chill factor, profess astonishment upon hearing it, and then demand a detailed scientific explanation of what it really means *vis a vis* the ambient temperature of the day. My response invariably is along the lines of, "Once it's below twenty below, who cares about the minor details?"

I've decided the best way to handle all future holiday calls is to prerecord a holiday message and send it in the mail. I'll get about five friends to all talk into the microphone at the same time while my dog is barking and my birds are squawking. It will sound exactly like a holiday call home. And about the same amount of real information will be shared. Best of all, I'll get to the feast before the maktak is gone.

Chapter 12

Cabin Fever – the heat that holds no warmth

When I came to Barrow in the early seventies, the Cold War was Wat its height. Distant Early Warning Stations (DEW Line Sites) were scattered across the Arctic as the first line of defense should the Soviet Union attempt an Arctic assault on America. Many of the sites were located in isolated areas where they represented the only human habitation for miles around. Others were located close to villages like Kaktovik, Pt. Lay and Wainwright. In Barrow we had something called POW Main, which is command center for the other, smaller sites.

POW Main is located behind the NARL airstrip about ten miles from town. Because it's a military installation, it can serve liquor despite the local ban on the sale of alcohol. When I first arrived, it also had a go-go cage.

You needed an invitation to get into the Site. That was not hard to come by if you were a nurse. Most staff at the DEW Line Sites were men and most nurses were women. Since DEW Line staff did not socialize with villagers, the hospital nurses and unmarried female schoolteachers had a standing invitation at the bar.

For many teachers and nurses, this was viewed as a safe place to let down their hair. Unfortunately, this led some to believe it was all right to dance in a go-go cage in a short skirt. Since there wasn't a man there who was going to object, many women who would otherwise have never realized this dream, actually got to strut their stuff like one of the Golddiggers. One of our DONs was infamous for her stints in the cage. Normally she was a reserved, older Southern woman. Put in the cage, she became a tempting tigress – at least in her own mind. To the rest of us, she resembled an older woman gone slightly mad.

The smaller DEW Line Sites were filled with the problems that inevitably arise when you plop six or eight men down in a very isolated, very cold environment for months at a time and ask them to look at radar screens 8 hours a day. Life consisted of work, watching videos on TV or playing pool, and sleeping. Since liquor was available at even the most isolated station, drinking became one way to cope. And since the people who volunteer for this kind of duty could be considered unique from the start, you often had some very interesting staff at these Sites.

I got to meet some of them when I went on a camping trip with some elders from Barrow and Nuiqsut. I tagged along while they worked with anthropologists and archeologists to map traditional land use sites on the Beaufort Sea near Nuiqsut at a place called Oliktok Point. I went because my camping buddy Sam had been hired as lead muscle for the group. He oversaw two other young men who came along to do the heavy work and hunt when necessary for the group. The project was sponsored by the Borough. They provided us with a skin boat and motor so we could cruise the coastline to get to various points of interest. Normally, a skin boat would not have been used in the fall but at the time there were no other boats available. Overland would have been a long, hard trek for the elders.

The campsite chosen was a subsistence cabin near Lonely, an aptly named DEW Line Site. Since they had an airstrip, it seemed logical to make camp near it for ease of moving gear and people. Our cabin was a small distance from the facility. We were clearly visible to them. The DEW Line Site itself consisted of about five connexes – metal boxes that look like they belong on a train – all strung together. Inside, the Site had all the comforts of home, including electricity, movie videos and steak and lobster dinners.

I arrived at Oliktok after the others had already set up camp. The three elders – Bessie Ericklook, a Nuiqsut lady and Luther and Cora Leavitt, a Barrow couple – slept in the cabin. An archeologist and his wife had their own tent. The anthropologist, Bessie's nephew Harry, a man named Robert from Barrow, and Sam, all occupied the same tent, sleeping in rather close formation. Imagine my surprise when I found out that I'd be joining them there. Just me and five guys in a tent on the edge of the Arctic. Possibly a dream come true were it not for the inordinate amount of clothing we wore all the time as the cold fall winds started their Arctic assault on the plants of summer.

The water on the Beaufort Sea was open. The snow was just beginning. In between the snow and wind, we had fog. On one of the few days deemed good enough for boat travel, we decided to try and reach a point of land not far from our camp where Bessie said she'd lived as a child. By the time we got there, the winds had picked up again and the weather had closed in.

It dawned on us all at about the same time that we would not be able to get back to camp that night. Luckily, there was a cabin nearby. Sadly, it was very, very small. We had limited food and gear for an overnight. Worst of all, we didn't have enough cigarettes to make it through the night. At this point, actual panic started setting in.

You need to understand that this happened before the great American smoke out. Over half the people on this trip smoked. Those that didn't soon wished they were on another plant altogether. We found some canned goods in the cabin since it was used off and on by various field researchers and that helped stretch our food supply. We even found some coffee. But what use was coffee without a cigarette. It's like having sex without an orgasm. It might be vaguely pleasant but it lacks sharp focus.

Eventually, the non-smokers grew testy about the level of agony being expressed. They suggested an early night leading to an early start in the morning if the weather was even minimally good. All the smokers quickly agreed. Anything to get us back to our stashed cartons in the cabin. We all took various pieces of the floor, table and chairs and tried to go to sleep.

What with all the shuffling and moaning sounds that emanate from a group of strangers sleeping in tight quarters, no one really got much sleep. So the smokers were semi-alert early the next morning when the unmistakable odor of cigarette smoke wafted by and gently teased our nostrils. Uncle Luther had found one last unfiltered cigarette butt somewhere in the depths of his gear. He'd lit up with a fresh cup of coffee.

The look on his face was sheer ecstasy. The other smokers gathered round and tried not to appear eager. We were about to put the Inupiat value of sharing to its ultimate test. Uncle Luther proved once again why he was one of the most respected whaling captains in Barrow. The strength of traditional Inupiat values came through for us. He passed it on so we could all have one puff. Bessie, being the oldest, got to go first. Protocol is always followed in traditional situations.

We finally decided that some things in life are just worth the risk and packed up to leave. We'd get back to Oliktok Point and our cigarettes using whatever means necessary. Sam and his helpers followed Uncle Luther's suggestion and built a shelter from canvas to cover the center of the boat where the women would sit while the men worked. Uncle Luther would guide and Sam would steer.

The shelter lasted about ten minutes. After that, so much ocean water washed over us with each wave that nothing could have been effective. Since the water was just a little cold – like around 40 degrees – each splash produced a thrill as it ran under your butt and down you hands and face. Yep, we were having fun now. Just to make it complete, the wind was blowing, the temperature was in the teens and I needed to go to the bathroom. It's what I always do in a crisis.

By the time we arrived back at camp, even I was beginning to doubt the wisdom of a habit that would drive me this close to death. Poor Bessie had fared even worse. We'd put her down in the bottom of the boat and tried to protect her from the worst of the cold and wet. She barely weighed a hundred pounds and looked quite frail. Of course, she was also an Inupiaq who had been brought up in this environment and knew what it took to survive.

Her legs had frozen in the crossed position in which she'd been sitting. She was soaking wet and shivering. I took her under one arm and one of the men took her under the other. We ran back to the cabin with her dangling between us, legs still frozen in a crossed position under her. The others had run back to the cabin to get the fire going. When we reached the door, the fire had just started and her bed was ready with all available blankets piled on it.

We gently laid Bessie down and started to cover her with blankets in an attempt to stop her shivering. Bessie impatiently pushed us away with surprising strength considering her condition and demanded, "Cigarette-mi" – which means exactly what it sounds like.

The weather started turning really bad soon after that and we found ourselves confined to the cabin for prolonged periods. Uncle Luther helped us pass the time by creating things as he told stories. We'd be so busy listening to some hunting tail from the past that we'd hardly notice his hands moving. Yet all the time he was talking, he was making something out of twigs and string and anything else close at hand. Once he made a ring game for us. He made a cross out of twigs, tied and looped some string around it and hung a ring on the string. Then he challenged us to move the ring from one side of the cross to the other on the string.

When birds started to bother the caribou carcass we'd hung up on a rack outside the cabin, he took some more twigs and strings and created a windmill to scare them. We placed it on the top of the drying rack and with the help of the constantly blowing wind, our meat was safe from seagulls looking for an easy snack.

Eventually, though, reality started to sink in. The weather continued to be bad and no planes came in to supply us. Soon we were down to our last pound of flour, our last bag of tea and – most worrisome of all – our last cigarettes. As any true Alaskan will tell you, those are three camping essentials without which there can be no quality of life.

Ignoring a warning voice in my head, I suggested we go across to the DEW Line and get some essentials to hold us over till the supply plane could land. No one seemed very eager to volunteer to go with me. In the two weeks we'd been camping next door, they'd certainly seen us enough to guess that we were probably not a threat to national security. The one person who'd come over to say hello – a man with the strange nickname of "Pyro" who cut a stove out of a barrel for us with a torch – seemed relatively OK. At least, he seemed OK if you ignored any possible connection between his nickname and his proficiency with a blowtorch.

I headed to the DEW Line with Owen, the archeologist. Imagine our surprise when the man who answered our prolonged knocking came to the door armed. I assumed there was some arcane military rule that required the doors to all DEW Line sites be answered armed. I figured as soon as he got a glimpse of Owen and me, he'd immediately laugh and offer us a friendly greeting. I was very, very wrong.

Not only would he not let us even get a foot up at the doorway so we could avoid the wind almost blowing us away, but he also refused to give us any supplies. It seems he had two problems with our request. One was a fear that if he did it for us he'd have to do it for everyone who decided to camp next door to his DEW Line and get stuck without supplies for a week. Two, his food was all federally registered down, apparently, to the last potato. How would he justify the missing items on his supply forms? This from the same military that brought you ten thousand dollar toilets seats and a coffee pot that could withstand the impact of a crashing jet so you could have coffee while you died. Somehow, I found his attitude unreasonable.

But that was nothing compared to Owen's reaction. Owen was one of the non-smokers. He had already spent one very uncomfortable night with smokers who had no cigarettes. He did not intend to do that again. I also think he was just a tad ticked off that he was being treated as the advance force for a Soviet invasion. Whatever combination of the two caused him to explode, I can only say that the East Coaster came out in him.

Although his tirade did not get us in the front door, it did get us some flour, tea and cigarettes. I think it also got our camp put on 24hour watch since the guy with the gun certainly seemed convinced we were a lost band of psychos out to cripple America's defense system.

I hear the military is computerizing the DEW Line Sites now. I think it's not a moment too soon.

Not too long after the Oliktok Point adventure, I found myself on a very small plane heading to a place called Tasiqpaq Lake. It's the largest fresh water lake in the Arctic and has some small cabins on its periphery used by various wildlife officials when doing caribou counts. It was the early 80s and I was running the municipal health department for the North Slope Borough. We were starting an Arctic "Outward Bound" adventure camp for young people.

⚜ PARALLEL LOGIC ⚜

The idea was to teach teenagers how to survive on the land using traditional Inupiaq skills they might not be learning at home due to family problems.

Although my job description seemed administrative, in the early days of the health department I found that the really relevant phrase in the job description was "all other duties as assigned". This came to mean a startling variety of tasks. When a complaint came in that someone had spent all winter emptying their honeybucket into an old wringer washer in their front yard, it was my responsibility to check it out and determine that yes, it did look like what it was purported to be. When it was determined that the kids on the summer city clean up crew could not be expected to pick up the dead dogs on the beach because of the maggots underneath the carcasses, the health director should. And if someone needed to go to the cabin on Tasiqpaq to check on its adequacy of space and supplies for the next Outward Bound group, I got to do it.

Two people accompanied me on the trip, which was arranged to cover a weekend – Carol, the lady to whom full responsibility for these trips would eventually be delegated, and that most famous of all Arctic hunters and campers, Sam. He was to be our guide and muscle. I think I selected him for the task based on the "hope springs eternal" axiom I had absorbed while trying to learn physics in college. Or perhaps parallel logic had struck again without my even noticing.

The only place for a plane to land was on the frozen lake itself. There was exactly one locally available plane that could do that. When the plane bent its prop taking off from the lake after depositing us there, our weekend turned into a week as the company waited for the new prop to be flown up from Fairbanks and installed on the plane.

It was the beginning of February, a particularly cold time to be camping in the Arctic. The sun was out about fifteen minutes a day. The cabin we shared was one small room with a tiny partition for the honeybucket. We had one lantern with limited fuel; limited food due to the fact that the first group of children had eaten five times more than expected; a box full of comics for our reading amusement; and no way to get away from each other unless we chose to hang around outside in forty below weather. It was the perfect setting for one of those mass murders where they find everyone dead and try to figure out who killed who first.

Since Sam and I were close friends who had camped together before, we were at least used to being with each other in close quarters over extended periods. Although this did not diminish my occasional desire to chase him to hell and back while screaming vile imprecations, it did mean we had both learned how to channel those impulses elsewhere for the good of everyone concerned.

In this case, I spent an inordinate amount of time making bread with no yeast. We had found approximately 99 pounds of flour but not one packet of yeast. Since we were very low on food, my bread became a staple of our diet. And since the loaves tended to be small and hard as a rock, they were also potential weapons should a wild animal attempt to enter our little sanctuary.

Carol, on the other hand, was an employee with whom I had not spent any prolonged periods of time. She had the more difficult task of spending a week in intimate circumstances with two people she did not know well at all. By the time we were rescued, she'd taken to standing on her head in the corner of the cabin stating that it relieved the pressure.

Aside from the flour, the only other food available was the limited supply we had brought for what we thought was a weekend's adventure and a bucket of caribou neck parts found on the step leading into the cabin. I combined the caribou parts with cup of soup contents and hoped for the best. Without potatoes or vegetables, salt and pepper became the predominant ingredients. Since we had no idea when we'd be rescued, we stretched it as long as possible by constantly adding water. By the end of the week, there was barely a hint that caribou had ever really graced the pot.

We occasionally saw caribou around the cabin. Carol and I felt Sam should go out and kill it for dinner. However, the skidoo was broken and he was loath to stalk the beast on foot unless we had truly reached the level of starvation. Sam seemed quite content to lie about in the cabin and read comics while munching on flat, hard bread slathered with the remnants of a jar of peanut butter.

Eventually, the walls of the cabin started creeping in on us at night while we slept. Soon the cabin was half its original size. There was not enough room to stretch your arms out when yawning without bumping into someone else's nose. It grew so close and tight that even Sam had to look up from his tenth reading of Donald Duck and notice. He decided to take action. The action involved him going out in forty below weather and chopping a four-foot deep hole in the lake ice so we could fish. It is probably significant that Carol and I spent more than one afternoon kneeling over this hole not caring if we caught anything so long as we didn't freeze to death or have to go back to the cabin. In the end, we caught nothing besides a little frostbite.

We had a portable radio with us in the cabin. What time was not spent at the ice hole was spent listening vainly for word that the plane was fixed and could come get us. My staff in Barrow, most of whom were known for their fairly warped sense of humor, kept sending song dedications to us over the local radio station. Songs like "Don't It Make My Brown Eyes Blue" dedicated to me from my dog Lovey. Songs that convinced me none of them would see a raise until well into the next decade.

Eventually, we were rescued. But not before the term "cabin fever" took on a whole new dimension in my life. I swore as I boarded the plane to leave Tasiqpaq that I would never again go camping without two very essential items – the complete works of Leo Tolstoy and a couple hundred yeast packets hidden all over my body.

Chapter 13

Cheese bar anyone?

By the late 1970's, I'd been director of the health department long enough to develop a healthy cynicism about the variety of federal and state programs purportedly designed to assist Native people. But due to my responsibilities, I often found myself in a position where I was forced to participate in them.

One of the hardest times I had with this was when the federal government decided to restrict caribou hunting. We were told not to worry. They would be providing meat to substitute for the caribou we could no longer hunt. The plan was for the feds to send beef up to the North Slope to be butchered at our local store and distributed to subsistence families affected by the restriction.

As with so many federal programs, the concept sounded a lot better than the reality. You have no idea how embarrassing it is to go to families in a subsistence village with two – that's right, two – pot roasts and announce this was from the federal government to make up for an entire winter's worth of caribou. I can only thank god for the inherent politeness of the Inupiat people. It kept them from laughing me right out of their homes.

Then, of course, we followed that brilliant moment with the great American cheese give away. This was Ronald Reagan's attempt to meet the needs of some of our more impoverished citizens. He thought it would be a good idea to take all the surplus cheese the government was buying from its farmers and redistribute it to poor families in need of healthy food. On paper, not a bad idea at all.

In reality, when handled by the federal government, a nightmare waiting to happen. And happen it did.

Someone miscalculated exactly how much cheese people on the North Slope could eat in one millennium. Five-pound bars of cheese started to arrive by the planeload. I remember getting so desperate I stood at the door to the Senior Citizen's Center and refused to let people leave unless they took some with them. I risked being personally responsible for constipating the entire elder population of Barrow – to say nothing of what this did to their cholesterol level.

I tried to convince whaling captains to use it as bait. We shipped it in hundred pound loads to the villages. We gave it away as prizes. We even used it as doorstops. And still there always seemed to be more.

Part of the problem with these food give away programs is that the people doing it are missing a central concept about food that anyone brought up in a deeply ethnic background learns at birth. There is no substitute for the foods of home. Food that is an integral part of childhood carries multiple layers of meaning and emotion. Nothing can ever replace that.

I felt the bureaucrats who thought they could blithely substitute a pot roast for whale meat should be dropped in one of our smaller villages for a winter. While there, they'd be allowed to eat nothing but subsistence foods. I'm willing to bet that at the end of the winter they'd have a much greater appreciation of the emotional content of our diet. Of course, I'm not sure we'd be able to get the Big Mac out of their mouths long enough to get a statement. But if we could, that's what they'd say.

It wasn't only the federal government, though, that impacted us with schemes and dreams. Often the most well meaning individuals would involve us in a plan we knew nothing about till it dropped in our laps. For instance, there was the time in 1976 or 77 when the boxes of furs started to arrive. Mink, fox, ermine – you name it and some object made from it was in the box.

A little investigation revealed that the boxes were coming from Mary Tyler Moore. She was spearheading a campaign to save animals from those who would kill them for their fur. Part of the campaign involved collecting those furs already sewn into coats, hats, stoles, etc., and sending them to people who had some valid claim to using them. Since Mary was a famous TV star, she and her friends had some pretty spiffy furs to send.

The cold of our winters qualified the Inupiat of the North Slope for the windfall. We had no warning before they started to arrive. At first, we were not sure what to do with them. In fact, my staff's initial reaction was that this was some kind of cruel hoax. By the time the third box was opened and a full-length mink coat fell out, even the most cynical of disbelievers became a convert. These people were serious. Serious enough to send coats that cost the equivalent of a year's salary for most of us.

Unfortunately, they were also relatively useless in the Arctic. Most mink coats do not have the kinds of ruffs and hoods meant to be worn on sleds being pulled by skidoos in forty below weather. So we called in all the women skin sewers in town and told them to have at it – make something useful out of this pile of ritzy skins.

The results were amazing. Within days parkys sprouted up in town made of gorgeous Hawaiian print materials lined with ranch mink fur. Mink hats were seen nodding piously in church. Children braved the arctic wind with ermine lined parkys covered in denim. And still the boxes arrived. It was as though someone had left the spigot opened and it was flowing with every fur-lined object known to man – plus a few we were having trouble identifying.

In fact, that soon became the problem. Even rich people apparently have a limited number of furs they are willing to send north. Soon the boxes started to contain totally unrecognizable objects. They may once have had real fur attached to them but then again, maybe not.

It was when they started to arrive smelling that I really got nervous. I don't think they smelled when they were packed. But somewhere along the way they had definitely stayed too long at the fair. I had this vision of headlines announcing how I had eliminated the entire skin sewing population of the North Slope through a diabolically planned scheme of strange rashes and disease caught from unidentified fur objects.

And then, just as mysteriously as they started, they stopped. No more boxes. No more excitement. No more ripping mink coats out of the hands of my staff while they muttered about being as old and needy as the next person. We had apparently sucked the well dry of every fur coat owned by anyone living within shouting distance of Mary Tyler Moore. For a little while though, we all looked absolutely enchanting in mink. Then we went gratefully back to our wolf and fox. At least we were sure of their etiology.

During my time in health, I also had occasion to host guests from the Soviet Union. Some came long before the exchange of visitors and information became so commonplace. In the early eighties, we had some Soviet physicians visit who were exploring how health care was being delivered in America's Arctic. They came with an interpreter who had little knowledge of medicine and was widely acknowledged as the KGB member of the group. If this was true, I can only say he must have had a very boring time of it.

The Soviet physicians were awed by the equipment we had at our local hospital. Since this was equipment we felt was old, out of date and in need of replacement, their reaction to it gave me a good idea of just how primitive health care was in the Soviet Arctic. Although conversation through the interpreter was a bit stilted, we were able to bring up subjects of mutual interest. I was particularly fascinated by their description of substance abuse in the Soviet Union in general and the Arctic in particular.

Basically, they took the attitude there was none. Or at least none to speak of. And certainly what there was involved alcohol, not drugs. And it was, of course, handled in a most efficient manner. At least, that's what they would have had you believe. As someone who's watched Native communities struggling with the problem of substance abuse for many years, I was more than a little cynical when I heard their explanation.

According to these physicians, if someone seemed to have a problem, it was reported to officials at his local workers' union. This official would pull the worker aside for a private chat. If that didn't work, he received a warning to straighten up. When all else failed, he was sent away to a "hospital" to be cured while his wages continued to be sent to his family to support them. Inquiries into the type of counseling available at these "hospitals" led me to believe that perhaps "work camp" would have been a more apt description. Needless to say, they claimed no one ever fell off the wagon after receiving the "cure".

PARALLEL LOGIC

But what these physicians lacked in credibility – and let's face it, if the interpreter was indeed KGB who can blame them for painting a rosy picture – they made up for in sheer charm. Their obvious delight in America was wonderful to behold. It was as if they'd been let loose in a gigantic Disney World.

The Soviets came with me to Barrow via Prudhoe Bay. This meant we had to fly in a small bush plane to get here. They were enchanted with the idea. Before boarding the plane, each stood in front of it for a photo. They'd never been on a plane this size before and viewed it as a delightful adventure. Luckily for them, we were flying with Beluga Bob, one of the world's most congenial bush pilots. He was so congenial, in fact, that he was able to communicate with the Soviets despite the language barrier and the fact that the interpreter and I had fallen asleep.

I found out about this communication when I awoke to find that one of the Soviet physicians was flying the plane. He had a grin as big as the sun splitting his face in two while he held control of the aircraft in his hands. Beluga Bob sat next to him with not a care in the world. After all, he had just given the guy a ten-minute explanation of how to fly a plane – all of it done through hand gestures – so he knew the guy could handle it. Had I felt equally as confident, perhaps I wouldn't have held on so tight I pulled the armrest up from the seat.

About ten years later, we had another group of visitors from the Far East. By this time, the myth of the Soviet monolith had collapsed and the visitors were no longer Soviets but Russians. The purpose of the visit was the same. They wanted to see how health care was delivered in the American Arctic – specifically, pediatric care since there were two pediatricians and a pediatric surgeon traveling through the auspices of the Institute for Circumpolar Health

As always with these visits, the physicians had a serious purpose and were exhaustive in their questions and interest in all areas of health care delivery. But even people as serious as they were needed some time to relax. So I made plans to take them on a tour of Barrow and its surrounding environs.

As a child of the cold war, my gut instinct as we approached the DEW Line Site was to deny it even existed. As a woman of the nineties, I was pretty sure none of the Russians had hidden cameras in their cigarette packs. It's one thing to read that the Cold War has been officially thawed. It's another thing to overturn forty years of air raid drills.

I think the final leg of my paranoia crumbled that day in the car. One of the physicians, Sasha, asked if he could drive for awhile. We were in the middle of nowhere – a place relatively easy to get to from Barrow – on a stretch of dirt called Gas Well Road.

After ascertaining through the interpreter that Sasha did indeed have a driver's license, I turned my car over to him on the theory he couldn't do much harm. The road was straight, there were no other cars to be seen, and the roadbed was at least seven feet across. Surely he could manage that.

My first indication of trouble came when he got in the driver's seat and started flailing his left foot all over the floor looking for the clutch. Only I didn't think far enough ahead to grasp the full implications of that move. Then, he couldn't get the gear shift to move out of park – a second warning that went right over my head.

If I think about it now, I realize that common sense should have told me that the Russian alphabet and our alphabet have little in common. Certainly R, D and N do not necessarily stand for the same things to them as to us. Especially if they have never before driven an automatic car. In fact, common sense would dictate that they would not even know to look for those little letters anywhere on the dash.

But since they live in a country that has nuclear weapons, I thought surely they would have automatic shift cars. I was very wrong.

After reaching over to show Sasha that he had to pull in a little on the gearshift to get it to move, he happily moved it down one and stepped on the gas. We zoomed backwards while experiencing severe whiplash. Not to worry though. When he realized what he'd done, he slammed on the brakes. He'd apparently never been near power brakes in his life either. As we whipped forward, all damage done by the backward whipping motion was neutralized.

Once we'd all stopped laughing and holding our necks, I gave a short explanation of automatic shifting. After that, the only real problem was his obvious delight in power steering – something else they had not yet achieved in Russian cars. Sasha was absolutely thrilled at how the smallest touch on the steering wheel sent us whipping back and forth across the road.

Once I got over an acute case of carsickness, I realized how glad I was that Sasha was no longer the enemy. Up close and personal, it's really hard to dislike someone who could make a Disney ride out of a short drive on a long dirt road.

Providing health care in the Bush has always been a challenge. But in the early days of the health department, it held some special challenges to the professionals recruited to start programs most others take for granted.

One of the first programs we contracted from Indian Health Service was the dental program. I was lucky enough to recruit a dentist, Jim, with both a sense of humor and sense of adventure. He also had a wife willing to put up with much adversity in order to stand by her man. Later, Janis grew older and a lot wiser.

We did not have clinics in our smaller villages that were capable of handling the space needed for a portable dental practice. Portable is the operative word here. There was nothing in the villages for the dentist to use. You brought everything with you from a portable dental chair with instruments to a portable autoclave. Mind you, some of this equipment did not necessarily start out life as portable. But if it was small enough to be carried, we added the word portable to its description.

Before the dentist went out to a village, he'd attempt to secure a place where he could set up his workstation. We quickly learned to not assume anything about the places we were allowed to use. For instance, we learned not to assume that the building would be heated – or that the room would not be full of snow.

Once Jim and Janis headed out to Wainwright on the assumption that the room we secured would be ready to set up the equipment and start work. When they got there, they found it full of snow with windows broken and no heat. Before seeing patients, they shoveled out the room, put visquine on the windows and got the loan of a portable heater. It gives new depth to the word dedication.

Jim and Janis were also the first dentist and assistant to make their home away from home in the jail cells of the new public safety facilities being built in our villages. Except for those times they were displaced by a real inmate, it had all the comforts of home. Well, at least it didn't have snow down the middle of the room.

Of course, getting to the village from the airport runway was a joy in and of itself. All the equipment had to be off loaded from the plane and on loaded to a sled and then pulled by skidoo to the village.

Jim often said the most discouraging part of his practice happened when he was leaving the village. Since dentists were not a regular sight in most of our villages until the Borough took over the program, dental health was – to put it mildly – shocking. Not only had dental care not been routinely available, but the diet of the Inupiat had been rapidly changing. Sugar from soda pop, candy and chips were a growing part of daily nutrition.

Jim and Janis would stand at the runway in sub-zero temperatures having just finished a week of 12 hours day. The plane would land and disgorge its cargo before they could load up to leave. Off the plane would come a thousand cases of soda. It's enough to make a dentist cry.

There were, of course, the fun times. While working in Pt. Lay, polar bear cubs were brought into the village. They'd been orphaned and the villagers were wondering what to do with them. A few phone calls later they were on their way to the Alaska Zoo in Anchorage. But not before Jim had gotten to hold them.

Years later, after he moved to Anchorage and had a family, he would bring his girls to the polar bear cage at the zoo and point out the bear he'd held. It may not work for long, but for a while, it made him bigger than Big Bird in the eyes of the only people that mattered, his daughters.

Another new innovation brought to the Slope by the expanded dental clinic was dentures. Due to the limited dental care provided by Indian Health Service, most people had one basic experience with the dentist – he pulled their teeth. With the advent of heavily sugared diets, teeth pulling became fairly common. If you lived in a village outside of Barrow, you were lucky if a dentist came through once a year. So you pulled your own teeth when they got too infected or painful.

I was always amazed by the two extremes apparent in our villages. Some people kept to a pretty solid subsistence diet and had fairly good teeth. Others ate a subsistence diet heavily interlaced with sugar – in soda, in tea (a minimum of three teaspoons per cup), in prepared foods, in candy bars, in the canned milk in their baby bottles – and at very early ages had few teeth left in their mouths.

Both Jim and I agreed that appearance can play a big part in how you feel about yourself. Some of the people with no teeth were quite young – many were in their twenties. As TV, radio and newspapers made an impact through the seventies, appearance became more of an issue than it might have been in the past. So, Jim decided what we needed to do was bring a denture clinic to the North Slope.

Having conquered the skills necessary to do ordinary dental work in extraordinary conditions, he thought it would be a small leap to bring dentures to all the villages. I think maybe he'd been inhaling a little too much leaking nitrous.

Bringing the denture clinic to Barrow was not too difficult. Of course, due to the costs involved in transplanting an entire lab on a plane, we had to compress the whole experience into one week. You had your teeth pulled on one visit. Then, when the denture clinic came to town, impressions were made. The lab tech then sat up all night baking the dentures and within 48 hours you had your first fitting. By the end of the week, you walked out with new teeth.

Words cannot describe the change dentures made in people's looks. Perhaps most importantly, words will never be adequate to describe the change to their smiles. It made all the hassle worth it. And never doubt it was a hassle, especially when we tried to move the process to even smaller villages.

The first village we tried to bring the denture clinic to, outside of Barrow, was Wainwright. The lab consisted of one very adventurous lab tech and a lot of equipment. The building was warm when they got there this time. They'd been there a couple of days when the following occurred.

They were working on a patient with dentures. They'd removed his dentures and put them in a cup of water next to the dental chair. As the procedure progressed, they noticed it was getting colder and colder in the clinic. Eventually they were seeing their breath on the air. But the procedure was important and they didn't want to stop. They finally got to the point where they had to put gloves on because their hands were so cold.

By the time they were doing dentistry in their parkys, Jim asked someone to check on the heat. He was told there was no fuel left. Seems someone in town had run out the night before and come over to the church building where the clinic was being held and drained the fuel drum. No one seemed overly concerned about this. After all, it was winter, it was the Arctic and the guy was cold.

So, dentistry proceeded in a rapidly cooling room while the word went out that they needed to find some replacement fuel for the clinic. Unfortunately, the procedure was completed before the fuel was found. Or, almost completed. The last step was to replace the dentures in the patient's mouth. As Jim reached behind him for the dentures, he hit something hard. It was ice. The water holding the dentures had frozen. The dentures were solidly frozen in the middle of the cup. It gave a whole new meaning to the words "Arctic dentistry".

After I left the Health Department, I worked as the supervisor of State Social Services on the North Slope. Basically, I was the chief baby snatcher in town. It was the early to mid eighties and the pipeline boom years hit our town hard. Anyone with a lick of sense would have realized this was not the time to go into child protective services and hope to come out with either sanity or health. As a devoted disciple of parallel logic, I am proud to say I have never had a lick of sense affect any of my major life decisions. So, I became the town social worker.

Part of the job involved being on call for emergencies. Since I was one of the first social workers ever hired here who had actually lived here before starting the job, I knew most of the people I'd be dealing with already. Whether they were cops, judges, lawyers or clients, we inevitably shared at least a passing acquaintance.

This became painfully evident to me after the first few middle of the night call outs. The police always accompanied the social worker on these calls to protect the worker from possibly angry or drunk family members who would object to the removal of the children from the home. Since this was almost always necessary, a police escort was routine.

Almost inevitably, I'd enter a home where a party had clearly been going on way too long. People would be passed out in various nooks and crannies. Some last diehards would still be attempting to get the bottle to their lips. And children would be running around, some watching TV, some sleeping, and some little babies badly in need of a diaper change. Since there was rarely an adult sober enough to be responsible for the children, I'd explain that the kids would have to come with me to an emergency Children's Receiving Home for the night. Then I'd leave a card with my name and number so that when everyone woke up the next day and realized the kids were gone, they would have some idea of who to call.

These removals apparently had been done in an atmosphere of tension and anger with past social workers so the police were primed and on alert. Then, just when they expected the blowup to happen, someone would yell out "Hey, Elise! How you doing? Ain't seen you in a long time. Come have a drink." This was, of course, uttered in a slow, slurred but happy voice. I could see the cops slowly turning to look at me in wonder. When I explained I'd be taking the kids, the cops would tense again sure that now the explosion would happen. Instead, someone would invariably say something like, "Hey, get the kids' coats. Elise is gonna take them home. Awright, Elise! We'll come get them tomorrow." And out the door we'd skip – me happy to have handled it without the children being subjected to any anger or fights and the cops staring at me with whole new levels of respect and wonder.

Of course, not everyone thought I was so wonderful. There were times when I had to answer a call myself if the cops were already on another call out. At times like that, I grabbed the nearest male friend who looked like he could defend me or – at a minimum – drive the get-a-way car. One such call came in while I was playing bridge. I grabbed my pilot buddy Beluga Bob – who had been a Green Beret or something like that – and told him to drive. When I arrived at the house, there were two old men sitting at a table very sober and obviously very distressed. There was a mom – granddaughter to one of the men – very drunk. She had her five-year-old daughter with her. She was chasing the child around the room, over sofas, beds and chairs while screaming drunken threats. The little girl was always one step ahead.

I tried to grab the child each time the circle came around to me and on about the fourth try was successful. I didn't feel this was the time to give my speech about where she'd be able to contact me or find her daughter the next day. From the look on mom's face, it was clear that I needed to move faster than I'd ever moved before if I didn't want my face ripped off. So I tossed the child to Bob who was standing in the doorway with his mouth agape. Unfortunately, mom – drunk as she was – was quicker. Before he could turn to go, she grabbed the arm of his leather jacket in a death grip. She did this by shoving her hand past my face and over my shoulder so that I was trapped between the two of them. It was in this fashion that we two-stepped out of the room – a mass of entangled humanity in total chaos.

Bob finally broke loose and I told him to get in the car and get the hell out of there with the girl. He was more than eager to comply. As he gunned the motor out of the driveway, I jumped in while the car was moving. Mom was but inches behind me. As the car picked up speed and we left her behind, Bob looked at me with a whole new level of respect in his eyes. I got the distinct impression, though, that he'd just scratched Social Worker off his list of future job possibilities.

Even more amusing was the time I went to pick up a 12-year-old boy who was late returning from a visit home. Since I knew the family had a long history of violence, I thought bringing a buddy along made sense. I felt silly calling the police for a simple pick up so I asked Kent, a houseparent at the Children's Receiving Home, to accompany me. He and his wife Ann had arrived in Barrow one day earlier. It was Christmas and they'd come up to fill in for the regular house-parents who were on vacation.

We drove up to the house and walked to the front door. I knocked. Kent squinted at a hole in the door and quietly said, "That looks just like a bullet hole". Before I could reply, someone cracked the door open just the slightest and asked what we wanted. I explained our mission. The door shut. Then the door opened again. As it did, we saw the business end of a rifle slowly emerge. I don't even remember getting back in the car I moved so fast.

Because of fun times like that, I was very happy to turn in my social worker hat after two years and put on the hat of City Recreation Director. I'd be in charge of basketball and softball leagues, bingo games and dances. There would be no on call emergencies, no guns pointed at me. I'd be able to go to the store and not be followed around by some angry parents calling me a variety of colorful names while I tried to decide which laundry detergent to use.

PARALLEL LOGIC

My first official day on the job was wonderful. I could handle these responsibilities with ease. I went home on singing feet. I went to bed happy to be alive. About 4 a.m. my phone rang. A voice asked me if Piurragvik (our rec center) had a football and/or basketball. Without hesitation – or any questioning about the nature of the inquiry at 4 a.m. – I responded in the affirmative. "Well, then", the voice continued, "would you please bring them to the emergency room of the hospital immediately."

Like an old warhorse, I responded without question. I leapt out of bed, dressed in thirty seconds, flew out to the car, convinced the wheels to turn even though it was about fifty below zero and the grease was frozen on the axle, grabbed the requested items and drove on to the hospital. I was about halfway there when it occurred to me to wonder why they needed these items at the hospital in the middle of the night.

My first thought was – when coherent thoughts actually re-entered my consciousness – it was a practical joke. But I couldn't imagine anyone I knew willing to risk what I would do to them if it was a joke. I got there to find out that there had been a shooting with a resultant large wound. They wanted to try using either the football or basketball to create enough pressure in the crater caused by the bullet to stop the bleeding.

As I left the hospital, I thought that in all the history of City Recreation and City Recreation Directors, this had to be the first, last and only time it would involve an emergency middle-of-the-night call out. Sometimes you can't win for trying.

Chapter 14

Cabinets – Small Rooms on a Cruise Ship

If there is any real symbol of the Arctic, it's not the polar bear or the northern lights. It's the house on skids moving down the road. People who come to the bush are generally nomadic, often loners. They've come here from there. They're looking to escape the hustle and bustle of urban life. Hell, rural life is more crowded than they like. So they keep as mobile as possible. You never know when civilization will rear its ugly head too close to you. Then you need to be able to pick your house up – literally – and move a little further down the road.

During my twenty years in Barrow, I've lived in just about every type of housing the Bush has to offer. At one point in the early years, my husband James and I moved into a house so small that when a guest was using the honeybucket, their knees bumped the knees of guests sitting on the couch. The only divider was a very thin curtain. You didn't miss any of the conversation when answering nature's call.

The guests sitting on the couch were also sitting in the living room and the bedroom closet. Giving a house tour was a very simple affair. You stood in the middle of the living room/ dining room/ kitchen/ guest room/ family room/ bathroom, and pointed to a divider while saying "That's the master bedroom". It was the easiest house to clean I've ever lived in. I could stand in the middle of it and reach all necessary surfaces with my sweeper and attachments.

What made me the most nuts about these Bush houses was that they were all designed by the same architect. He was a man. Of this

I have absolutely no doubt. He thought cabinets were the small rooms on a cruise ship. He thought storage was a woman's job and not one he should have to worry about. He assumed it was a woman's greatest joy to stand in the middle of a three-bedroom house with a handful of sheets and bath towels while wondering how to arrange them so they looked like a living work of art.

When I started designing the house I'd eventually build, I had very few absolutes in mind. One was that the bathroom would not look like a spittoon with bucket. It would be big enough to turn around in without serious injury to the kneecap. It would have a medicine cabinet that could hold more than a tube of toothpaste and one toothbrush.

This hang-up was due to many sad experiences with bathrooms in early Bush housing. For instance, there is the never to be forgotten moment when you find out that your house has no bathroom. For painfully clear reasons, outhouses are not an option here.

When you're raised in the lower '48, you pretty much assume every house has a bathroom. In the Arctic, this was not necessarily true. What almost every house does have is a corner that can be converted to a bathroom by the placement of a honeybucket in its center.

Friends of mine, Dave and Sarah, rented a one-room house that had started life as a storage cache. You can imagine how big it was. In case you're wondering how you convert a cache into a house, it's actually very simple. You put a big tin bowl on a stand and – voila! – you have your kitchen. Then you take a honeybucket and place it in some out of the way corner of your spacious abode and – yes, you guessed it – a bathroom.

In David and Sarah's case, the only corner available for this was next to the refrigerator and under the bar on which they hung their clothes. There was no room for a curtain. However, if they tastefully arranged one of Sarah's longer skirts, they could provide themselves with a modicum of cover. Ultimately, they depended on the discretion of others in the room.

In some houses, you ended up using odd little spaces you found to substitute as a bathroom. In one house I rented with my husband, there was a little closet-like space that stuck out from the kitchen/living room. I hung a curtain, placed a honeybucket and bowl in it, and felt like I was living in the lap of luxury.

PARALLEL LOGIC

The only problem was that we moved into the house in the summer. Even though summer may not hold the same meaning in the Arctic as it does in Hawaii, at least it's pretty consistently above freezing. And it's always above zero. So it wasn't till winter set in that the truth became evident. In a house with minimal insulation in general, my new "bathroom" had none. By November, the ice had built up waist high. By the end of the winter, going to the bathroom resembled entering an ice cave.

I moved the bowl out when the water starting freezing every morning. It made washing my face a true "wake-up" experience. First, I broke through the ice – if that was in fact possible – then I took a deep breath, splashed it on my face and wished like hell I was in Hawaii. On those days when I felt compelled to wash my hair, I'd boil up water, place it in a pitcher and learn how to wash and rinse in less water than I now use to brush my teeth. Necessity is truly the mother of invention.

An even more moving experience, though, was answering nature's call first thing in the morning. By January, this went way beyond an uncomfortable but necessary experience. It moved into the realm of indescribable, you-had-to-be-there, there-are-no-words, type of moment. It hovered over parallel logic like an amputated limb – its ghostly presence could be sensed but its reality could not be touched.

I'd roll out of my warm bed to have my feet touch a floor only slightly above freezing. I'd put on slippers that made not the tiniest bit of difference in how cold my feet were. I'd hip hop madly to the one throw rug in the living room area. I'd stop there for a moment to regain my sense of balance and breath. During this moment, I again wondered why I had not continued west on my journey, past Seattle and on to the Pacific.

When feeling returned to the bottom of my feet, I made another mad dash – this one to the bathroom. Once there, I'd automatically sit on the bucket only to shoot up like a gas-fueled flame a nanosecond later. This was because the honeybucket – and all its contents – were solidly frozen.

It's like a religious experience – until it's actually happened to you, your imagination can provide but a pale facsimile of the real thing. Having shot straight up from the seat, my mind instantly clicked into survival mode and I remembered that I was supposed to hover over – as opposed to sit on – the honeybucket in winter. One of the advantages of this experience, of course, was that I didn't need coffee to get going in the morning. By the time I emerged from the bathroom, I was definitely wide-awake. I was also having deep doubts about the sanity of life in the north.

At one point, I tried to emulate my friend Sonya and insisted to my husband that we install a gas toilet. Unfortunately, the one we bought was designed for people with very small functions. Anything over a teaspoon of liquid or a cigar's worth of solid matter overloaded its capacity. If you had company, this was quite a problem since they spent most of their time trying to burn and re-burn the material they'd left behind. A trip to the bathroom could take about two hours. This seriously cut into conversation and dinnertime.

I felt I'd really moved into luxury when we rented a house with a real sink area. Of course, the pipes ended abruptly right under it. A bucket was placed beneath the pipes. The sink water drained in the bucket and you periodically emptied the bucket out. If you forgot to empty it, you quickly remembered when fairly gross and smelly water started to seep out from under the sink on to your foot.

Besides adequate bathroom space, another absolute in the design of my dream house was that it have enough closets, cabinets and varied other storage space to satisfy twenty years of pent-up frustration. I can still remember the day in 1978 when I inspected the new Borough house I'd been assigned. I went through it like a kid in a candy shop. Here were actual rooms with doors. There was carpeting on the floor. There was a definable bathroom. It had a strange object in it – one with a seat and water in an area that was actually heated. It had another strange object in it – long, curved, white, with water that came out of a tap. If I wasn't so sure such things no longer existed, I'd have guessed it was a tub with shower. There was a kitchen with a sink whose pipes did not suffer from abruptus interruptus. I felt as though I'd again entered the world of parallel logic – this might look real but couldn't possibly be true.

I left the house and went back to my office with a big grin on my face. I was moving into a house that resembled my childhood home. Even if my pipes ended in a tank that had to be pumped, at least I had pipes. Yet through all this joy, something niggled at the back of my consciousness. Something was out of place. I kept trying to convince myself I just wasn't used to the sight of plumbing or windows that really opened. But that wasn't it.

Suddenly it struck me. That mysterious Bush architect had struck again. I'd just walked through a three-bedroom house in which there was not one closet. Oh sure, there were four whole cabinets in my kitchen. But that was the beginning and end of storage space. Each bedroom in the house had a three-foot long shelf on one wall with a bar hung underneath it. Process of elimination led me to believe that this was, in fact, some sicko's idea of a closet substitute.

There was no linen closet; there were no clothes closets – no, not in any of the three bedrooms. The bathroom had a medicine cabinet that had clearly been designed before people had medicine therefore making it superfluous to allot it any amount of space. The kitchen had the aforementioned four cabinets, which had to hold a winter's worth of canned and boxed food stuffs as well as all pots, pans, dishes and cleaning supplies.

I must admit there was a good-sized qannitchaq. The qannitchaq not only constitutes a cold storage porch, but by having a door that leads into a small, unheated room and thence to your actual front door, you keep the Arctic wind from sucking all the heat out of your house every time you open and shut it. Over time, this Arctic entry way expanded into a cold storage porch. You could leave you winter's worth of meat out there and it would stay frozen till June. You could store anything that freezing wouldn't affect so long as you remembered that its freezing may affect you.

For instance, a qannitchaq could be used to store your tools like hammers, screwdrivers and wrenches. Freezing temperatures don't affect them. But freezing temperatures will wreak havoc on your hands if you don't give the tools time to warm up when you bring them in to use. Gripping a solidly frozen metal wrench handle is another one of those moments the Arctic offers in such quantity – a "you had to be there" kind of moment. It was doubly important to remember to warm up the tool if you were pressing a friend into manual labor in your home. Friendships can be made and lost over very simple things. Handing a friend – who is already under your sink and wondering why he's there if he's not married – a wrench that has just come in from a porch where the temperature is 40 degrees below zero is apt to be one of those simple things.

Unfortunately, this qannitchaq did not have any shelves in it. They were all in the bedrooms disguised as closets. So everything sat on the floor. By mid-winter, everything was frozen to the floor. It would remain that way till May or June – tantalizingly in sight but clearly out of reach.

The house also had a large water tank in a utility room just off the kitchen. A water truck would make deliveries once a week and a sanitation truck would pump my waste tank routinely. Compared to carrying out full honeybuckets to empty in fifty-gallon metal drums, this was heaven. But as always with government projects, they're never quite complete. As the water and sanitation system improved, the Borough came back to my house and retrofitted it for the latest version of whatever system we were using that year. One time through, they attached my tank to a water line that allowed me to automatically fill the tank myself. This gave me more freedom than I'd had in years when it came to water consumption. At a time when we were paying about 11 cents per gallon for water, my monthly bill quickly shot over $150/month.

Unfortunately, not all of that money was being spent on water actually used towards a positive end. A lot of the money was being spent on water that ended up cascading over my water tank, on to my floor and thence down a path in my kitchen where it always started to freeze when it encountered the front door. This occurred because there was no gauge on my water tank. When I went to fill it, it was strictly by the guess method – "I guess it needs water now", "I guess it's full now", "I guess that sound is not a waterfall on TV but my water tank overflowing again".

The pipe carrying water to the tank went in about mid level on the tank. The only accessible hole in the tank was at the very top – about two inches from the ceiling. This was the hole the waterman had used before the advent of piped water into my house. Joe the Waterman – and he will always and forever be known as that – had a knack for knowing by sound just how full the tank was. I'd stand there, knocking on the side of the tank, pretending in vain that I heard a difference between the full and empty portions of it.

I eventually hit on the idea of climbing up on a chair next to the tank and holding the handle end of a wooden spoon in the hole at the top. When I felt the water hit the spoon handle, I knew there was enough water in the tank. We won't go into how many wooden spoons I lost in that tank. I only hope that wood has nutritional value. If I remember rightly, Ewell Gibbons thought it did.

I also hope that socks and gloves have nutritional value. Sam had a habit of hanging his wet work gloves and socks over pipes at the top of the ceiling. Occasionally when he went to retrieve them, one would be missing. I chose not to think about where they went so long as people who drank my water were not being rushed en masse to the hospital emergency room.

Actually, I liked it when Joe was delivering water to me. He was not only consistently cheerful, but he was actually known to make statements like "Thank you for being sober". This was during the boon years of the pipeline when lots of money and jobs were flowing through town. So was lots of alcohol and drugs. It was a rough time for our little community. We lost many good friends and watched many of our families get damaged. Those of us working in the health field walked around with a permanent sense of guilt that we couldn't do more about the problem. Not being miracle workers, in the end we did our best to patch together those we could.

Through all these years, Joe the Waterman delivered water to homes with every type of water system you could imagine. He delivered in every kind of weather possible and never wore a coat. One of the more indescribable sights in this world is Joe jumping out of his water truck in 70 below weather with a blizzard blowing wearing nothing but boots, jeans, T-shirt and orange work gloves. He says a coat gets in his way when he's jumping in and out of the truck so much.

After serving Barrow for over ten years, including the boom time, Joe has many priceless stories about delivering water late at night on pay day weekends. He has been known to use his hose as a weapon, turning it on those he'd come to serve who were drunk and threatening him. And he's been known to suck all the water back out of the tanks of people who just pushed too many of his buttons. Once, he sprayed water all over the front door of some particularly obnoxious people and froze it shut. Water can be an awesome weapon in forty below weather.

Chapter 15

Polar Bears Go First

My first spring whaling season in Barrow, a young girl named Sandra took me out to whale camp. I was new to the Arctic and still viewed the world through urban eyes. As long as there was no one around who looked like they planned to mug me, I figured I was relatively safe. So I accepted her invitation without hesitation.

Spring whaling is done on the pack ice. The whalers wait for a lead to open up and then camp there. A lead is open water where the pack ice has split. Since whales are mammals, they have to come up for air to breathe while migrating. They follow the leads on their way to the Beaufort Sea.

The pack ice is relatively unstable. You'll be at camp on the edge of the lead when you'll suddenly notice the ice you're standing on is waving under your feet. It is starting to break apart. If camp is on the wrong side of the break – the sea-side instead of the land-side – everyone scrambles into action. I've seen entire camps with equipment, skidoos, skin boats and sleds, broken down and moved in about ten minutes. And sometimes that's not even fast enough. Often the last skidoo has to leap over a steadily widening bridge of water to get to the land fast side with the last sled.

But I didn't know all this my first time out. There were no muggers in sight so I figured I was extremely safe. Going down on the ice for the first time is always a memorable experience – especially if you're from a big, noisy city. You enter a world of total white-blue silence. The only sound you hear when the skidoo engine is off is the sound of the ice creaking and moaning. It's like being in a sensory deprivation chamber except instead of being deprived, your senses are filled with alien sounds. Nothing is familiar.

I was absolutely entranced. In between, I feared for my life. Not because of the usual things – as I said, there were no muggers and few other humans were encountered. Only the occasional sled going back to town for some supplies. No, what scared me was the trail we were on. What scared me was the idea that someone actually thought this was a trail.

The ice builds up on the pack throughout the winter for a variety of reasons. One of the results of that build up are areas called ice or pressure ridges. These are large mountains of ice that have been squished up by the movement of the sea under the ice. To get to the open lead, you have to cross them. This has to be done fairly carefully since a skin boat (*umiaq*) must be hauled across the path without being torn to shreds by jagged ice edges.

So whaling crews carve trails up and over these ridges at the best possible spot, creating a path that only the foolhardy would really consider a trail. You find yourself going up over a ridge with only a foot or so on either side of you. You have to be careful about stepping off the sled because the snow often hides a deep crack in the ice that will easily swallow your foot and leg. As you come hurtling down the other side, you find yourself facing another wall of ice as the skidoo cuts a sharp ninety degree turn and you pray to god the sled cleanly follows.

Needless to say, one of the first things I learned about going to whale camp was this. If you're sitting on the sled, hold on no matter what. By virtue of their construction, even if they do turn over, they'll just turn on their side. Its rare for them to actually do a three sixty. Of course, this advice is a lot easier to accept when you are standing on firm ground than when the sled is turning over amidst walls of jagged ice.

The other advice I received was that if I was on the back of the sled steering it – a euphemism for hanging on for dear life while swinging your body weight from one side to the other in the vain hope of averting disaster – I should abandon it the minute it started its turn. I soon perceived that it was not at all wise to mix these two pieces of wisdom up.

So Sandra and I started out for my first trip to whale camp with me in blissful ignorance and Sandra exuding the confidence of youth. We arrived at our destination in relatively good shape. Nothing much was happening at the time. Some men were watching the lead for whales. Others were in the tent resting, playing cards, snacking. Sandra and I were soon quite bored and decided to take a walk. We made this decision independent of any reasonable advice from the whalers.

Because of the particular make up of the ice that year, there was about a ten-foot ledge of new ice formed at the edge of the lead. Because it was new, it wasn't very thick. You could look down and see the water moving under it. We decided this would make a great place to walk. With the bliss born of innocence and ignorance, we followed this ice all the way to the next camp – about two miles away.

When the people at the next camp saw our approach, they seemed a lot more concerned than I thought was warranted. After all, we were safe. We'd just taken a pleasant stroll on an icy path. Within minutes of our arrival, we were being treated to a stern lecture from the whaling captain about polar bears and unstable ice. Up till then it hadn't really occurred to me that polar bears lived on this ice. Polar bears lived in the Bronx Zoo. They were cute and almost cuddly.

A few days later, word came from the ice that a polar bear had torn up one of the camps and almost destroyed a skidoo. I had a retroactive anxiety attack.

Over the years, I've come to accept the fact that polar bears don't only live in the Bronx Zoo. And I've come to accept that they do more than play in the water and look cute. Here, in their native habitat, they are much more awesome and noble looking than in the zoo. They are also much more fearsome and deadly.

When I first arrived on the North Slope, polar bears had been hunted to the point of being endangered. They were placed under federal protection through the Marine Mammal Protection Act. Only subsistence hunters could kill them. Any non-native who killed a polar bear would have to be able to prove the bear was causing immediate danger to life and there was no other option but to shoot.

Under these circumstances, the polar bear population rebounded with vigor. Soon, we had them as regular visitors not only at whale camps but also at our dumps and in our back yards. It became almost humdrum to hear about the mom and cubs seen near the Post Office late at night. So long as they were gone before I went to get my mail, who cared?

After all, I'd lived in New York City. I knew what real danger was all about. And as news drifted up here from various urban areas of the country, I soon came to view polar bears as the much lesser of many problems to be faced in a modern world. I just figured that New York had its muggers. Chicago had the wind. L.A. had its drive by shootings. And Barrow had polar bears wandering the streets in search of the perfect snack. All in all, a fair trade.

Until that fall when we harvested over ten whales on the beach. Traditional subsistence whalers on the North Slope work under a quota system. The quota is developed at International Whaling Commission meetings after much hard work on the part of the Inupiat and scientists to provide the best census data for the whale population. If they don't fill their quota with spring whaling, they whale again in the fall. The difference is that in the fall the ice is out and the shore has open water. The whalers use slightly bigger boats in the open seas of fall – never an *umiaq*. And they bring the whale right back to the beach to harvest. You don't have to travel to the edge of the ice to help.

This makes it a lot easier to participate in the fall harvest. Anyone can walk down to the beach and offer a helping hand. But it also means a lot of tasty smelling debris left behind for polar bears to sense. No matter how thorough you are in harvesting a whale – and the Inupiat are about as efficient as you get when it comes to wasting nothing – there's a carcass left at the end with some tasty morsels dangling from it.

During this particularly successful fall whaling season, polar bears were strolling our beaches like movie stars at Cannes. They seemed to take over the whole beach. While they had lots of scraps to eat, they were fairly innocuous. No matter how much the whalers tried to clean up and cover the harvest area, still the bears came.

In their wake came some of the most insanely stupid human behavior I have ever witnessed in a race with a supposed degree of intelligence. Word spread quickly through town that all you had to do was jump in your car and drive towards NARL and the Point to find polar bears wandering in groups of up to two and three feasting on whale remnants. And so people did just that. They jumped in their cars and went to stare at these masters of their icy universe.

The ice was so far out to sea we couldn't even see it on the horizon. Yet still these bears came – swimming long miles in frigid waters to reach the treats. Of course, the bears didn't consider the water that cold. They live their lives out on the Arctic pack ice except for occasional forays to land.

Any time a bear gets used to being around people, you can pretty much figure his death warrant has been signed. In this case, we had lots of polar bears feeding on lots of whale scraps. They were fed and content. They ignored the people around them. Once the food was gone, though, they wouldn't come across as such Yogi Bear types. They'd eye every person nearby as a potential entree in the evening meal.

Once a bear loses his fear of humans, it is only a matter of time before a tragedy strikes. All too often, the bear pays for human errors. In this case, some of these people watching them were not only guilty of errors but – much more onerous in my mind – they were guilty of a level of ignorance that boggles the mind. The phrase "Too stupid to live" played gently in my ear.

People would drive out to the beach where the bears were feeding on the whale carcass. They'd bring their kids and a camera. They'd stop the car near a bear eating and let the kids out. Then, at a distance of maybe fifteen feet, they'd place the kids into a little group and back up to take a shot. This left their children alone and unprotected within 15 feet of a feeding bear known for some fairly unpredictable behavior if annoyed.

The potential for future disaster for both bears and humans led the Borough's Wildlife Management staff to try a series of tactics to scare the bears away and cause them to associate people with discomfort. They used loud noises and gunshots to try and drive them back into the sea and away from town. Meanwhile, the Borough launched an all out effort to clean up the beach area so no morsels would be left to tempt them back. As always happens, some bears lost their lives because they would not be frightened away. Most decided the picnic was over and headed back to the ice to see what else they could find for dinner.

While all this was going on, Barrow was visited by a movie producer. Catherine Wilder had come to scout some possible locations for a movie she was considering. As the Borough's Public Information Officer, I got to show her around. I was thrilled. I may not have been too familiar with her work, but I was a devoted follower of her late father, Director Billy Wilder, and his movies.

She was interested in seeing some of the northern coastline. I arranged for us to go out by helicopter to survey the area. It was mid fall. The sun was slowly setting for its winter nap and the snow and ice were fresh and clean. It made for some pretty spectacular light as the sun bounced low off the horizon on a world of crystal gleam.

As we flew over the newly frozen land, the pilot – an old time Arctic hand – said he might have something special to show us. Talk about your basic under-statement. One minute the chopper is smoothly gliding over the new ice of the Beaufort Sea and the next minute we're hovering over about eighteen bears munching on what looked like a frozen whale carcass.

It's highly unusual to see more than a mom and maybe two cubs together at any given time. Polar bears are solitary creatures. Theirs is not the herd mentality. Yet, when a feast such as this is laid out for their delectation, they will munch together peacefully till their bellies are full.

It was hard to tell what kind of whale they were eating because the ice had frozen up all around the carcass except for the abdominal cavity. The bears had eaten down into the cavity so far that they were actually lying in the bloodied hole they made as they continued to feast. When the noise of the helicopter startled them and made them run, they emerged from the carcass with their whole bottom half covered in blood. They had literally become red and white bears.

They ran about ten yards, stopped, looked up at us with some disdain and returned to their feast. All around them on the ice were white foxes patiently waiting their turn. They gave us a glance after their initial startled movement and then also chose to ignore us. They settled back in their previous positions of silent sentries – the waiting circle.

I envied them in a way. They belonged in nature in a way that man stopped belonging a long time ago. The white of the ice extended to the white of the fox and bear in a seamless flow. Even the bright red of the bears' bottom halves couldn't mar the flow.

They're part of the fabric of the wild – not intrusive, not apart. The Inupiat, when engaged in traditional hunting on this ice, become another thread in that fabric.

I remember a friend commenting on how well adapted the Inupiaq are when on the ice hunting compared to some of the awkwardness evidenced in non-traditional settings. Until you've seen people on their own turf, you really shouldn't judge them.

Having seen polar bears on their own turf, I felt very comfortable judging them as beautiful but not friendly. I was quite content to keep a comfortable distance between us. However, since my office was in a building on the bluffs overlooking the Chukchi Sea, polar bears were frequently on my mind. As the ice freezes fast to shore and the sun sinks below the horizon for the last time, seemingly friendly places can take on a sinister air. Our office was in a quiet section of the beach and it was not unthinkable that a bear might come off the ice and up the cliff to explore for some kibbles.

In fact, one day at lunchtime, even before the ice came in and froze to shore, two friends came by our office to pick someone up for lunch. As Chris and Harris sat there waiting, Chris noticed something swimming in the water. It was a bear. It was a bear with a mission. He was swimming hell bent for shore. Chris and Harris alerted Public Safety and they showed up to observe the scene. However, since the Marine Mammal Protection Act is still law, they were helpless to do much more than observe unless the bear threatened someone.

The bear climbed up the cliff outside our office window and headed for a bluff where a couple of dogs were staked. The dogs reacted predictably. They immediately asked for a permit to carry nuclear weapons. Since no one wanted to see the dogs get hurt, some shots were fired to scare the bear off. More shots and noisemakers were brought into play as everyone tried to convince the bear to go back to where he came from for his own sake.

He paid us absolutely no never mind. He ran back along the cliffs, passed our office windows and on into a more inhabited part of town. Eventually, the word went out for an Inupiat hunter to come and dispatch the intruder since no other means of dissuading him seemed to be working.

Now what was most funny about this incident was that two staff from my office were eating lunch at work while all this excitement transpired outside our doors. At one point, one of the two said something to the effect that there sure seemed to be a lot of noise outside. She wondered aloud what it could be. She went to the window to check it out and found herself watching a polar bear run by her nose with a variety of people in different stages of pursuit.

I had this story in my head as winter set in and I was frequently the first person at the office. I'd park next to the dark, frozen ice of the ocean and sit in silence while I anxiously checked all around to make sure none of the white stuff surrounding me was going to attack. Then, when I felt it was minimally safe, I'd leap from the car and run to the front door with the key in my outstretched hand ready to turn the lock. Once inside, I would slam the door, heave a sigh of relief and then feel pretty foolish. Even bears won't eat writers if there is anything else available.

However, one day something happened that forever changed my attitude about feeling foolish. As the sun made one of its last feeble attempts to rise slightly over the horizon, my boss Marie casually said to me, "Did you see those fresh polar bear tracks on the ice outside?"

Well no, I hadn't. If I had, I'd probably not felt so comfortable alone in the office that morning. Sure enough, a quick check showed tracks coming in from the ocean ice and heading straight up the bluff to our office. The Inupiat say they've seen polar bears drag dead walrus carcasses out of a hole in the ocean ice using just the strength of their front paws and arms. A dead walrus means about a ton of dead animal. Our office door would be no challenge. My car would be nothing more than a nuisance to be overcome while getting to the goodies inside.

So now when I get to work early, I wait at the corner for someone else to show up first. If they make it in safely, I follow. I view it as the Bush equivalent of the urban hassle of a traffic-clogged commute. In my case, the polar bears have right of way.

Chapter 16

The Midnight Sun Snowball Tournament

Sports are taken seriously in the Arctic. When I first arrived here, the only place to socialize outside of the Polar Bear Theater was at the City League basketball games. It was simply the place to be seen.

Each year, businesses in town would sponsor a team. Some sponsors actually put money into the league by buying uniforms for the players. Some lent their name and little else. For many teams, the closest they could come to a uniform was to try and coordinate wearing about the same color T-shirt so that their teammates could recognize them on the court and not inadvertently throw the ball to the wrong player. Since the city had precious little money, an admission fee was charged to defray the expenses of buying a basketball or two and possibly having trophies for the end of the year tournament.

It was at these basketball games that I first realized just how different things were done up here than I'd been used to in the lower '48. For instance, children came to all social events and pretty much were allowed to roam freely. It was understood that if they fell, started crying or got in a fight, the nearest adult would deal with the situation. It didn't matter if you knew them or not – though in Barrow in 1972 it was highly unlikely there was anyone you didn't know. Coming from New York, it took me quite awhile to get used to the easy familiarity that everyone here has with every one else's life.

It was also at these games that I was first introduced to the intensity of the athletes in this town when it came to their sport. It was not something joked about. Basketball is second only to God here – and I suspect god herself is surprised she's still clinging to the number one spot.

Many years later, when I spent a brief moment as Recreation Director for the City of Barrow, I found out the true depth of that feeling. I remember standing in open-mouthed awe as the captain of one of the teams – a friend in any other circumstance – actually accused me of deliberately scheduling his team to play the 9 p.m. games so they'd always be tired and lose.

I don't know what amazed me more – that he thought I cared enough about the whole thing to bother trying to engineer something like that, or that he actually thought I had enough understanding of the process to manipulate a basketball league schedule. Either way, it was at that moment I realized most of these guys could handle castration jokes easier than they could handle the idea of someone messing around with the game schedule.

And while basketball players are notorious in their own special way, nothing can outdo the fanaticism of those who play softball. Softball had been played here for a long time, but it wasn't until the late seventies that it took on a dimension that made many basketball complaints look reasonable. I guess if you think about it, there has to be something a little strange about people who willingly play ball outside while it's snowing and the temperature is hovering around twenty degrees with fog you could lose your family in.

We actually have a field in Barrow dedicated solely to the pursuit of softball. The fact that this makes it viable about two and one half months a year – if we're lucky and it's a mild spring followed by a late fall – bothers absolutely no one. In the winter, you can see some of the more fanatical players passing the field in their cars, looking longingly at where the pitcher would stand if ten feet of snow hadn't covered it.

By late spring, they go by with increasing frequency, measuring the diminishing height of the snowdrifts. This is a good indicator of when the field can be plowed of the remains of winter and readied for the official start of the season, the annual Midnight Sun Round Robin One Pitch Marathon Tournament that occurs on Memorial Day Weekend. This tournament is called off only if the blizzard is so bad

PARALLEL LOGIC

that the outfielders are in danger of disappearing into drifts searching for a ball. Even then, it's not called off because of danger to the players. It's only called off to avoid the arguments over how many bases the runner can take if the ball is never recovered.

My first memories of the Bobby Fischer Memorial Field, named after a local bush pilot, come from before they put gravel on it and actually made it flat. Originally, it was used just as nature had created it. This meant there were all kinds of interesting bumps and lumps. Balls would fall into puddles so intimidating that a local rule was created saying if the ball went in certain puddles, the player got an automatic two bases and no one had to try and retrieve it. It's disheartening for cheering fans to see their team's outfielders all standing around a mud hole saying, "You go!" "No, I went the last time. It's your turn to look for it." "Oh yeah, well, I have to go home now." This rule avoided those types of embarrassing scenes.

Another interesting moment caused by the bumpy contours of the land was something we refer to as a "really bad bounce". This means the ball has hit some small hill in the middle of the field, changed directions completely and is heading back towards home plate all by itself. The interesting rule question here is this, "If the catcher grabs the ball and tags the runner out but the ball had never actually been touched by an outfielder because the bounce sent it back in, is it an out or do we all just get to go home and have an aspirin?"

Since those days, the field has been smoothed out and the league has organized independently of the City Recreation Department. A little hut has been built with a concession area downstairs (read a room with a counter and one electric outlet) and a scorer's booth upstairs.

For reasons I have never quite figured out, I was one day offered the privilege of co-broadcasting a weekly game on the local radio station during the season.

My two partners always call the game since they actually know something about it. I'm there for "local color". What that means is I fill in the dead air in between exciting times on the field. It's an exercise that's made my life immensely interesting. You really don't know what live broadcasting is all about till you've tried to fill in fifteen minutes of dead air time caused by the fact that the second baseperson lost her contact lens in the gravel of the field. Both teams joined in the search. It was an awe inspiring gesture of good will but – as anyone who has ever lost a contact anywhere can tell you – a basically futile gesture. Be that as it may, we still held up the game for fifteen minutes looking for it.

Our hookup to the radio station in town is somewhat primitive by most standards. We call them up and broadcast over the phone. In recent years, we actually had a dedicated phone line put in for the purpose. This set up means you can't hear what's happening on the radio while you're on the air. So Earl Finkler, Barrow's answer to Harry Carey even if no one can remember the question, brings a little transistor along with him. This lets us know if we're really on the air or not. This is an important piece of equipment for our broadcasts since we have been known to do over 30 minutes of superb softball commentary only to find out we'd been talking to ourselves.

The other commentator – our play-by-play man – is named Bob Thomas. He pretty much waves good-by to his family at the end of May and moves into the booth for the duration of the season. His family periodically sends pictures of the kids so he'll remember what they look like come the end of August. Bob is infamous for being able to call the plays in the thickest of fogs or snowstorms. This is because he knows the teams and players so well that he can tell who made a play by the color of the coat or parka they're wearing. This is not easy when the person is playing wrapped up in a coat with a hood pulled over his or her head and a muffler hiding their face.

Bob is also a frightening storehouse of all the trivia you ever wanted to know about any team playing in the Barrow league. We'll be on the air in the middle of a game and Bob will be keeping the official score, working the scoreboard and announcing the play-by-play all at the same time. Just for the hell of it, I'll ask him some question about a team's standing or stats to see if I can stump him. He always has the answer without looking through any of his books. Of course, since there's no one to dispute what he says, for all I know he's been making it up all these years and has us all conned.

Bob was an involuntary part of one of my craziest on air moments – an honorable achievement considering the insanity that is a routine part of my Saturday morning "Discount Radio" show. That show is billed as having no standards so there is nothing to fall below. Since that show is a non-paying, volunteer program, it has given new meaning to the term, "You get what you pay for!"

When broadcast of each game draws to a close – either because the game is actually over or because we've run out of air time – we turn it back to the announcer at the station. This means the announcer must not only be there but he or she must be paying attention to the broadcast to hear us say the words, "And now back to (insert announcer's name) at KBRW."

The day this particular problem occurred, Earl was out of town and only Bob and I announced the game. When it ended, Bob left me to wrap things up while he went down to get the field ready for the next game. I cheerily wrapped up the statistics on the game just ended, announced the game to come, thanked every one for listening and said those famous words, "And now back to Isaac at KBRW". Then I took my headset off and turned the transistor radio up to make sure Isaac had heard and taken it back at the studio.

I did this casually, almost nonchalantly. After all, someone had always been there. Only this time, I was greeted with dead silence. I checked the radio to make sure it was on and the volume turned up. Then I checked the dial. We only have one radio station up here so it was unlikely it was turned to a different channel but I wanted to be sure I was really hearing dead air. And sure enough, I was.

I quickly plugged the portable equipment back in and went back on the air. One thing that had been drilled into me from the start of my career as a volunteer announcer with KBRW is that you never left dead air. While "Discount Radio" may have defied all statistics in that area due to my inability to master anything electronic, I sincerely did try to avoid it when possible. I announced again that the game was over and, with a slightly pleading tone to my voice, begged Isaac to take it back.

With each plea, I would whip my headset off and turn up the volume on the radio to see if there was a response. I was always greeted with dead air. I had no music to play. No material to read. No action on the field except for Bob going around making chalk lines to the bases and no one in the booth with me to fill in the time. I was desperate. Then my eyes fell on Bob's dinner, delivered earlier from his family.

Desperate times call for desperate measures. In what has to be an all time low in my broadcasting career – and this includes all those New Year's Eves on the beach describing fire works – I found myself giving a detailed description of his dinner. I actually spent a full minute describing the texture and color of the lettuce on his cheeseburger. My reasoning was that if I was bad enough on the air, people would go over to the radio station in desperation and pound on the door till Isaac woke up and got me off the air.

Ten minutes later I was still on the air and reaching the hysterical stage. I found myself begging anyone who might be listening to go over to the station and rouse Isaac. After fifteen of the longest and deadliest minutes of my life – during which time I actually described, in minute detail, the condition of my fingernails – I heard Isaac come on the air. I've never been so happy to hear someone in my entire life!

Because softball is so popular, there are enough teams in a town of 3500 to have four games a night five nights a week not counting the kids. We have men's league, women's league, coed league and the league that uses the really big softball for those who have no idea what they're doing but want a reason to be outside in the summer. The fact that it often snows during our Fourth of July games discourages no one. The same people often play in three different leagues.

Although I've managed to avoid ever playing the game, except for one short season in which I proved beyond a shadow of a doubt why I don't play, I did once own a team. It was called "Elise's Barrow Beauties". Unfortunately, shortly after its birth I was fired from my job and lost my ability to continue financial sponsorship of the team. Luckily, a local honeybucket service in town (whose motto was "We Clean Up Your Act") took over where I left off. The name of the company was "Elephant Pot Sewage" and their mascot was a pink elephant sitting on a honeybucket.

They continued to use the name Barrow Beauties and became famous for causing the development of two new local rules. One was a time limit on the games. This occurred after one game that started at 9:30 p.m. and didn't end until after 1 a.m. Since this is the Land of the Midnight Sun, there was enough light to allow the game to be drawn out to its natural conclusion. The final score was 31 to 0. It had taken over four hours to complete seven innings.

PARALLEL LOGIC

Another such lopsided competition led to the "ten run rule". This one states that if one team is ten runs ahead of the other after five innings, the game is automatically over. Then, just to make things more complicated, a rule was instituted that said if you were ten runs ahead and it wasn't yet the fifth inning, when it was your turn to bat next, you could only have two more batters after a run was scored and then the inning was over for you even if you had no outs. Or something to that effect. It was an effort to make the games at least slightly competitive while giving everyone a chance to not be completely humiliated.

My favorite local rule is the one that says if you play for one of the better teams, you can only have a certain number of home runs per game. After that, for every home run hit you get called out. It makes for a very interesting game.

That is definitely one of the good points about local leagues. When you eliminate those players — male and female alike — whose testosterone has gone nuts, you are left with a large group of people who want to have a good time while getting some fresh air and exercise. These people believe that having a good time and getting to play and enjoy the game is actually more important than winning. They are actually able to admit that this is Barrow softball and not the World Series. For some of our more competitive players, that statement is heresy.

I think the image that wraps up the real meaning of Barrow softball for me occurred about ten years ago. One of the players was my friend Charlotte, a nurse from the hospital. Charlotte was a bit older than most of the players on the field. But she had more enthusiasm, agility and speed than many a couch potato half her age.

She played for the Barrow Beauties. Her usual position was far out in right field. It was a quiet place and one that would not be hard for a "sixtyish" woman. These people obviously just didn't understand Charlotte. In all the years I've known her, challenge has never scared her. If something was hard, she just worked a little harder at it. Even now, well into her seventies, she lives alone in a cabin outside of Homer and skis about a mile to her mailbox every day. Something as silly as a softball was not going to intimidate her.

After many games of standing in right field waiting for the hit that never happened, her big moment finally came. It was a typical Beauties' games. They had not a snowball's chance in hell of winning but they were having much too good of a time to notice. Charlotte was standing out in right field bundled up and ready for action. There were two outs. The batter took a swing and hit a high, long ball down the right field line. It was headed straight for Charlotte. The entire crowd – players, umps and fans – held their collective breath as she backed up to get under it while shading her eyes from the sun.

And then, just when it seemed as though we could hold our breath no longer, she caught it. I don't know who was more surprised, Charlotte or us. The field erupted in one long roar as both teams took the field to carry her in on their shoulders. And carry her in they did, accompanied by the sound of the crowd chanting her name. It may not have been a major moment in softball history around the world. But for Barrow, it defined what the game was all about.

The Beauties have moved up in the world now. They are no longer sponsored by the distaff end of life but are now proudly owned by Fran Tate of Pepe's Restaurant. This means free food after they win a game. This incentive has done them well. It's no longer a news flash when they win a game. They are no longer the inspiration for new rules designed to end the game within the same season it began. And they rarely lose by 30 points anymore.

A new sport that has taken hold among some of the more insane here is running. While running is an honorable sport in most of the world, I still find it difficult to understand the allure of getting dressed up in eighteen layers of clothes, face swaddled in mufflers and masks, in order to run in twenty below weather while ice forms and freezes on whatever facial protuberance is not fully swathed.

Running is, of course, an old and time-honored tradition here in some ways. When dog teams were the primary means of transportation, people often ran beside them. One of the great Inupiat feasts called "Kivgiq" involved foot races between the host's representatives and representatives of the invited guests. And, of course, pretty much everyone has heard of Clair Okpeaha, by deed if not name. He's the Inupiat man who ran fifteen miles to Barrow to tell the missionaries about the plane with two white men that crashed near the camp where he and his partners were hunting. The men were Will Rogers and Wiley Post.

PARALLEL LOGIC

But once mechanization occurred in the form of skidoos, most Inupiat were happy to take advantage of the ease of travel it provided and few thought it necessary to run beside the skidoo. Of course, there was that time my ex-husband was hunting and jumped off his skidoo to shoot at caribou. Unfortunately, the throttle was stuck and the skidoo took off without him. He chased it a distance while yelling something that sounded like "Stop, you SOB or I'll shoot you!" The skidoo didn't stop so he shot it. His explanation for this action was that if it wasn't going to come back to him he was going to kill it. Luckily, he missed. Since the skis had been turned slightly when he jumped off, the skidoo eventually made a slow, wide turn and came back to him. Like with a cowboy's horse, the loyalty of a good skidoo cannot be measured.

One of the most valiant and faithful runners in Barrow is my old broadcast partner Earl Finkler. He may not be the best runner in the world. In fact, he may not be among the top 10,000 fastest runners. But if heart and willingness count, he's definitely among the top ten.

Earl organizes something euphemistically called a "fun run" that occurs on Saturdays throughout the year no matter what the temperature. This run is used to celebrate such wondrous events as the last day the sun sets in November and the first day it rises at the end of January. He says it keeps him in shape and forces him to run on days when he might otherwise be tempted to lay about and do nothing. He also claims that he could be close to first in the run except that he's being polite and hanging behind to make sure none of the stragglers get lost. Considering the run is done on Fresh Water Lake road, a fairly straight shot from here to there with no real turns or trees to obscure the path, some find this a questionable statement.

But for those of us who know Earl as the courtly gentleman he really is, we can only say, "Well, yeah, maybe it is a questionable statement but who else is willing to organize a 'fun run-walk-hop-skip-jump-crawl-bike-a-thon' in below zero weather because of concern over your coronary functioning?" One of the main rules of the run is that it is considered the height of rudeness to make it to the lake, then go circle back around Earl and then back to the lake, especially if you're walking.

I've seen joggers running up here in weather so cold it would be cruel to leave a snowball out in it; their faces so covered in ice and snow they look like Hieronymous Bosch's rendering of frost come to life. Their breath freezes on the air as they exhale and then they run into it and breathe it again. Yet they swear that it's fun. Which only goes to prove that in this world, there is truly something for everyone.

And if there is any doubt at all in your mind about that statement, then you need to attend the Barrow Christmas games and wipe those doubts away.

The Christmas games are held between Christmas and New Year's. The start on the twenty-sixth and end with an Eskimo dance on the first. The Inupiat here dance to celebrate just about all occasions of life. The dances range from very stylized, occasion specific ones to general, everyone participates dances.

The games are traditional tests of strength and skill. To an outsider, they can seem somewhat bizarre and painful. After you've been here awhile and have gotten to know the people and culture, they don't seem so bizarre anymore though they continue to be painful.

Just to give you an idea of what we're discussing, the names of the various competitions range from the "knuckle hop" – which is every bit as painful as it sounds – to the one man carry – which consists of a bunch of people hanging off one person like bananas on a stalk while that person tries to see how far he can walk. The competition is held between the married and the single, men and women vying separately.

Then we have the various pulls that range from the understandable if painful – such as finger and leg pulls – to the absolutely too painful to look at such as the ear pulls. In the ear pulls – since I know I heard you all ask what they were at the same time – a string is wrapped around your ear lobe and that of your opponent. You then pull as hard as you can until one of you gives up or you pull an ear off. Luckily, most people give up short of acquiring the Van Gogh look but often not before getting bloody.

When I first came here, I felt I should at least try one of the games just to confirm my original suspicion that I was meant to be more spectator than participant. Since I was nursing at the time, I decided to try the finger pulls. Between giving injections and wrestling recalcitrant E.R. patients, I felt they'd be pretty strong.

In these particular pulls, you hold a stick between two fingertips. The stick is attached by string to a similar stick your opponent is holding between the same two fingertips of her hand. Then you pull like hell until one pulls it away from the other. You then change hands and do it again. Best two out of three takes it.

Since life here is casual even during contests, the games are somewhat relaxed about rules. Insofar as possible, there are few to none. If a married woman is sitting in the circle waiting to be challenged, any unmarried woman in the audience can get up, go sit in front of her and thus challenge her. Whoever is defeated, leaves the floor and then the waiting begins again for someone from the other team to challenge the winner.

In these games, anyone who shows up to watch becomes part of either the married or single team and can challenge the opposition. If no one goes down on the floor to challenge the person sitting there after what is considered an appropriate amount of time, the competition is declared closed and the last person on the floor claims the victory. At the end of the games, the side with the most points wins. They get a flag.

I sat down in the center during the finger pull competition only half understanding what was happening. I'd only been here a few months and really didn't know what the games were about. But I was fairly successful in fighting off the competition and when the games ended for the night, I was still in the center. I mistakenly thought this meant I'd won and I could now go home and rest on my laurels.

I quickly found out that what it meant was that I had to return the next day and continue to meet all challengers until there were none left who wanted a piece of the action.

By the next day, I was beginning to feel the effects of the pull on my fingers. It felt like I had crippling arthritis. The idea of going back to the competition held all the appeal of a root canal without anesthesia. But this was my new home and I wanted to make a good impression – or at least not look like a cowardly bad sport – so I returned to the center of the floor.

Apparently word had gone out the night before that some new nurse looked to take the finger pull competition from the locals. In order to not have this happen, a formidable group of married women lined up to challenge me. I looked up at my first challenger. Her eyes were cold and hard. I realized I not only didn't have a snowball's chance in hell of winning, I would consider myself lucky if I got out alive.

Ever since that time, I've enjoyed the games as a spectator but have had little to no desire to compete. I like my fingers right where they are with no swelling, dislocation or pain to interfere with their activities. It's just a silly quirk I have.

Chapter 17

Adeline – She never met a man she didn't like

It's hard to explain how an animal that molts eleven months out of the year and has a mouth that would make Lenny Bruce proud can get under your skin. But Adeline got to me and never let go. She died after eighteen years as my constant, if somewhat strange, companion. She died on my kitchen table while being treated by our vets. Seems she had a liver problem. In retrospect, I'm not surprised.

Adeline liked alcohol. It was that plain and simple. Since I've never been much of a drinker – I fall asleep after two drinks or throw up after one beer – it's not something we shared. But it was something she shared with many of the men in my life. I can remember coming home from work and finding her on my husband's shoulder while he had a beer. Every time he put the can to his lips, she'd stick her head between his face and the can and pull the can towards her until she got a drink. There were many times in my marriage where she shared a lot more with my husband than I did.

The first winter I spent in Barrow was pretty rough. I was devastated with loneliness. I'd left my love, my family, my friends, everything familiar. The only thing I had nearby to remind me of home was Adeline. Adeline had a very definite personality. She made it clear that she preferred men to women any day. She also made it clear that she had certain expectations about her life with me. My failure to fulfill these expectations would leave her no choice but to dive bomb my carpet with her droppings. Trying to keep her caged up was only minimally successful since I lived in an apartment and the neighbors preferred not to have the quiet of the night pierced with Tarzan-like shrieks.

Despite all this, we were close. I'd sit there in my living room that first winter writing long, plaintive missives home. She'd stand on my head and try to cheer me up with her chatter. If I refused to be diverted from my task, she'd lower herself in front of my eyes by holding on to my hair and sliding down my face. When she had too much to drink, she'd stand sullenly on the bottom of the cage, unable to hold on to her perch. If I made too much noise, she'd growl at me. Not at all unlike many of the men I dated except they didn't have the good taste to go stand in the bottom of a cage.

If I was eating dinner and she wanted some, she'd fly to the table, walk up to my dinner plate and daintily nibble her way around the items that pleased her. She was always a hit at my dinner parties.

Adeline also had guts. No one and no thing was ever going to intimidate her. When my next-door neighbor got a St. Bernard, the dog evinced considerable interest in Adeline. More interest and familiarity than Adeline liked. She made her usual hissing sound that served as warning she was getting really pissed. Qimmiq, a wonderfully friendly but perhaps not so bright dog, did not heed the message. While Qimmiq's mistress and I worried that he might seriously harm Adeline if allowed to get too near, the real danger was to Qimmiq. One day he did get too near. Adeline came charging down the side of her cage and bit him on the nose. He turned tail and ran out of the living room yelping.

From that day forward, whenever he came to visit, he'd come as far as the living room and stop dead in his tracks. He'd then stick his head cautiously in the room and sniff. The minute he got a whiff of Adeline he'd freeze. There was no moving him any further.

Qimmiq was actually a key player in one of the funniest dinner parties I ever attended. His owners, George (of owl and walrus fame) and Sonya, were holding a dinner party featuring a standing rib roast for which they'd mortgaged their future. It was stunning and done to perfection. George carved the ribs and laid a beautiful slab of meat on each guest's plate. He carved a few extra pieces, and then went into the living room to join his guests. The roast was left on the kitchen table with all the other accouterments to the meal.

As people finished their first serving, Sonya and George urged them to have more. Most said yes and eagerly headed for a refill. After awhile, Sonya and George noticed that no one was having seconds on the rib roast. Afraid that people were just trying to be polite and not eat all their meat, they reiterated their invitation to have seconds on everything – including the meat.

Finally, one of the guests admitted they'd love seconds but were unable to find the roast. Sure enough, it was missing from the table. And Qimmiq was being extraordinarily quiet. By the time he was located, he'd just finished off about fifty dollars worth of prime rib. There was a smile on his face and a belch on his breath. It probably says something about how George and Sonya felt about Qimmiq that their only reaction to the fiasco was laughter.

My buddy Sam, despite being George's brother, never quite had the same feeling for animals. He viewed the menagerie that was my home as the price to pay for free lodging. Most of my animals were quite content to live in peaceful, if parallel, co-existence with him. Except for Adeline. It just really bugged her that there was a man she couldn't conquer.

One day, after many years of parallel existence with Sam, Adeline was on my shoulder as he and I played cribbage. She was muttering under her breath, always a sign something was on her mind. Sam and I were sitting across the kitchen table from each other. We both had our arms propped on it. Adeline was making tentative forays down my arm towards the table and then running back up my shoulder. I knew she was getting ready to do something but I had no idea what it was. Sam was keeping a close eye on her activities, giving her a baleful stare whenever possible.

Suddenly, she dashed down my arm and ran across the table to where Sam had placed his arm. She froze for a moment. So did Sam and I. She cocked her head up at him as if to gauge his character. Sam stared down at her. And then, very quickly but deliberately, she ran up his arm to his elbow, held her position for a second and then ran back down, across the table and onto my arm. She'd made her point.

Another moment involving Adeline that will always stand out in my mind was the day we had a birthday party for my husband. We'd made chocolate cake. This being the end of the sixties, when pot was still a prevalent part of the youth culture, the cake had a little extra zing baked into it. It was Sunday afternoon and a group had gathered at our house to celebrate. When the cake was served, Adeline was included.

By the time my in-laws dropped by for an almost unexpected visit, everyone in the room was pretty happy and silly as only good cake can do for you. When we saw the car pulling up, we hid the pot cake and brought out the spare cake kept for just such a possibility. We all pulled ourselves together as best as possible, sat the in-laws down and put on some water for tea.

My mother-in-law was sitting next to Adeline's cage. Up to that point, I hadn't really been paying much attention to the bird. But now she caught my eye in a very definite fashion. She was standing on her perch swaying from side to side and cooing like a drunken sailor. Clearly Adeline was in a very good space. She was enjoying herself and didn't care who knew.

I saw my mother-in-law eyeing her closely. I quickly intervened and said something to the effect that Adeline hadn't been feeling too good of late and that was why she was acting funny. "Something she ate", I muttered in desperation. By now Adeline was swinging with vigor. Her head was whipping from side to side with an enthusiasm that seemed to belie any illness. And then she threw up.

Not a polite little gurgle into the bottom of the cage. No, she used the whipping motion of her head like centrifugal force and launched that brown blob right onto my mother-in-law's lap. I should have known then that the marriage was doomed.

Before Adeline died, I acquired two other birds – a bare-eyed cockatoo and a Red Lored Amazon parrot. Both came to me through a woman, Mary, who actually ran a pet/flower shop in Barrow. Considering the average temperature here, this was either a very brave or very foolhardy idea. It would later turn out she had a sideline not quite as legitimate as the shop that kept her in bird kibbles.

The first go round with her shop – and there would be quite a few – occurred when I was still health director and so was forced into more than passing interest in her enterprise. For instance, there was the Thanksgiving she brought up the live turkey for a raffle. This is an idea that's better conceptually than reality would warrant. By Thanksgiving, the temperatures here pretty much preclude having the turkey scratch for feed in your front yard. The idea that she was raffling a live turkey for someone to take home was not one I wished to dwell on for any length of time. Les, our indomitable vet, cheerily took on the task of seeing to it that the turkey was mercifully dispatched before it left the store.

Of course, the turkey was not the only out of place critter to ever come through this town. There was once a very large pet snake owned by a schoolteacher who left it each summer to be cared for by his house sitters. He left a couple of rats to be fed to said snake whenever it woke up and looked hungry. Most of the time, the snake lived a somnolent life in a cage. For some reason, the young men house-sitting one summer decided that the most efficient way to handle the chore was to leave the two rats in the cage with the snake so that they'd be there whenever he woke up hungry.

The rats initially cowered with fear in a corner of the cage. Eventually though, they noticed that their dreaded enemy was pretty much sleeping off his last meal and not paying them no never mind. So they relaxed a bit. Then they relaxed a little bit more. Soon they were so relaxed about their situation that they felt very comfortable chewing their way through the snake while he slept. When the house sitters returned from work one day, they found two well fed rats and a snake chewed in two.

We've also had people attempt to re-create a lower '48 Easter by bringing up chickens, ducks and rabbits. Since the weather had usually climbed above zero by the time they were big enough to put outside, these animals didn't become a problem until fall when freeze up began. One year, the Borough Housing Director received complaints about noise and odor emanating from an apartment whose tenants were away on a long trip. She went in to find that they'd left their chickens inside the apartment. Well, after all, you couldn't expect them to live out in the cold. The destruction that can be wrought by a few chickens on their own in an apartment for a couple of weeks is apparently amazing. So is the smell.

But the oddest story of all has to be the one about an electrician walking down the streets of town one day only to find a parrot walking up the street towards him. The parrot was quite tame or quite cold. Whichever it was, he let the man pick him up and carry him home with nary a peep of protest. Extensive advertising on the radio brought not a shred of evidence concerning ownership. It makes you wonder, doesn't it? How do you not notice your parrot missing? At any rate, the electrician acquired a life long friend.

My second parrot, Captain, came to me via Mary and her pet shop. He'd been living there for about a year chained to a perch with no cage around him. The kids had tormented him enough that the sight of hands and fingers sent him into a tizzy. They hadn't meant to be cruel, but a young bird doesn't understand their interest in trying to touch him.

Mary was closing the shop in its first incarnation and couldn't sell him. So being the bleeding heart liberal I was, I took him. Initially, Captain and Adeline spent a good deal of time trying to de-feather each other. Eventually a strong bond grew between them and they were able to occupy the same cage without the presence of the National Guard.

Captain never trusted people the way Adeline did. He wanted to be brave and strong. He wanted to be friendly. At least, that's what I told myself. But the sight of a hand coming anywhere near him made him go nuts. Since it's hard to scratch his head or offer your shoulder as a perch without your hands being somewhat in evidence, he never quite achieved Adeline's ease with the human race.

Perhaps the most interesting moment I ever had with Captain came about 3 a.m. one Sunday morning. I was young then. Staying up late didn't necessarily incapacitate me for the rest of the week. As I sat munching on a bowl of cereal and promising myself this would be the last chapter of the book I'd read before going to bed, motion from the birdcage caught the corner of my eye. It was very steady and rhythmic. It was interspersed with strange little chirping sounds. I looked up to discover that Captain was standing on one foot while the other foot was draped coyly over the perch. He was rubbing his butt up and down on the perch. His wing feathers were arched in a cape around his shoulders. He was quite intent on this activity and seemed to have shut the rest of the world out. Adeline was in a corner pointedly ignoring him.

After observing his activity for about two minutes, it occurred to me that there was only one real explanation for what I was seeing. It's just not something I'd ever heard of birds doing – in or out of captivity. Even as I decided it was late and I was probably just hallucinating

– something I'd never actually done on pot before – Captain started making little sneezing like noises and arched his wing feathers till they almost entirely covered him. If it wasn't a bird orgasm, it was definitely the next best thing.

I decided not to tell anyone about this little episode for fear they'd finally and irrevocably have me declared unfit to live alone with animals. Besides, it was 3 a.m. and there was a chance it had all been a figment of my imagination.

I watched Captain closely over the next few days and saw no repeat of this activity. Eventually I forgot about it except for momentary stray thoughts about it being time to finally give up pot.

At the time this episode occurred, my dentist friend Jim was living in Barrow. His house being close to mine, he often came over in the morning for a cup of coffee and ride to work. One morning, as I was in the bathroom combing my hair while Jim sat in the kitchen, I heard him call out to me, "Elise, come quick. Look at what your bird's doing! What IS your bird doing?"

I don't know if I was more relieved to find out I hadn't been hallucinating or embarrassed to find out that Jim thought the bird was doing exactly the same thing as I thought he was doing. Having broken the ice, Captain seemed to feel no compunction to hide his behavior any longer. I can't tell you how many smart parties were stopped cold in their tracks due to this little habit. I'd be sitting there in my living room entertaining some friends when I'd notice a growing silence starting near the birdcage. I knew without a doubt what was causing the silence. As though to avoid even the slightest possibility of this activity being misinterpreted, Captain perfected his act so that at the critical moment, something that looked like a little miniature penis would emerge from his bottom and shoot god-knows-what across the cage.

Some would watch in awe and wonder. Others watched in total disgust. Depending on the group that was gathered, this activity would either lead into very interesting discussions of sex and the single bird or very embarrassed attempts to find a topic that would avoid any mention of what had just happened.

Eventually I got used to the fact that this was a routine part of Captain's life. Adeline made the necessary adjustments also. So long as he wasn't hitting on her, she didn't care what he did to his side of the perch.

Then, just when Captain and Adeline called a truce in their relationship, I acquired CB, a Bare-Eyed Cockatoo. She also came from Mary during another time when the store was being closed and she was leaving town. I first saw CB when he was living in the body of a grandfather clock. Not exactly spacious accommodations. She needed a home. And even though Mary assured me her accommodations were not as small as they seemed because whenever Mary was home CB was allowed out of the clock, I couldn't walk away from her. So I ended up with yet another bird in my life.

While Adeline was alive, Captain had a model that showed him he could be friendly with humans and not fear for his life. Not that he ever did anything with that knowledge. As for CB, she wasn't even interested in the idea. She considered herself the aristocrat of the group and spent most of her time distancing herself from the lower class of bird with which she was forced to coexist. I'd watch the three of them in action and think how really graceful CB was. If this had been England, CB would have been in the House of Lords and Captain and Adeline would have defined the lowest common denominator in the House of Commons.

When they flew, CB would weave graceful arcs and hover daintily over the perch before making a gentle landing. Captain and Adeline would lumber about like overloaded cargo planes and land with a thud that shook the cage.

After Adeline died, Captain went into about a year of mourning. Eventually, he bonded with CB but never to the extent that he did with Adeline. Unfortunately, Adeline's death also caused a direct regression in any social skills Captain may have been acquiring. CB never even attempted those skills. Unless I have food in my hand, they have one reaction to my approach – they hiss.

Eventually, I turned to professional publications for help. I read one article that said if I threw a towel over them, wrapped them tightly, then scratched a certain point on the back of their heads, they would eventually coo in blissful submission. Apparently, they'd never read the article. When I tried it, they spewed green liquid while spinning their heads entirely around on their necks. The only result of the effort was that they took to eyeing me like extras from Hitchcock's "The Birds".

PARALLEL LOGIC

For the longest time after I tried this method, they would glare and hiss every time I drew near. In between, they would act hostile. As I'd suspected, ten years of progress had been totally negated. Some friends – and I use the word advisedly – suggested that for the amount of progress made in ten years, the amount of backsliding was hardly noticeable. Others suggested that when I found myself begging for the friendship of a cockatoo and parrot, it was time to reassess my social life.

I tried spending huge sums of money on various cages for them in the hopes of buying their friendship. I was finally reduced to finding a cage whose edges did not provide a perch for target practice on my carpet. Every time I thought I had the problem solved, they'd prove they could lean out just a little further than before and still hit the carpet.

When I finally moved them to linoleum, they took to using my dog for target practice. As he wandered around their cage scarfing up every bit of food dropped, they'd follow carefully until they were positioned directly above him and then let loose. There is nothing quite as pathetic as the sight of your dog totally unaware he is covered in bird droppings running to greet you when you come home from work.

One cage I bought for them had acrylic sides. The manufacturer assured me there was no way they could stand on the edge because there was nothing for their feet to grip. My birds took this as a personal challenge.

As I watched a friend put this particular cage together, both birds watched with a look that would have frightened me had I not been so desperate to stop the target practice. Once the new cage was assembled, I took all the food and water from the old one and transferred it to the new one. Then I spent the better part of three hours begging them to move.

Finally, I took charge of the situation – if only to stop my friend's hysterical laughter – lifted up the perch they were on and dumped them in the new cage. Talk about excitement!

The initial looks they gave me can be summed up in one word. It is not a word I use in polite company. As I removed the old cage from sight, the looks turned really ugly. I'm glad they didn't have weapons or the hands to use them.

Then the struggle began. Captain had always been a bully with CB. Now, the worst of his bully traits came shining through. He made her life miserable by pecking at her, screaming and refusing to share the food or water. Since there were three separate dishes in the cage for this purpose, it took all his energy to run from one to the other while protecting what he clearly viewed as his turf.

Things finally came to a head about three days later. We had spent an extremely tense weekend. CB had climbed all about the new cage and seemed to thoroughly enjoy it. Captain had gone from bad to worse. And then he pecked at CB once too often. I came out of my chair screaming. I went up into his face and we had a conversation beak to nose. I was louder.

I'm guessing this is not an approved method for training and handling birds. On the other hand, my blood pressure did drop and Captain decided maybe he'd give the new cage a chance.

It didn't work, though. Seems that with just a little effort, birds can grip acrylic and climb up the side of sheer, smooth wall. Don't ask how. Like a belief in god, it's just one of those things you learn to accept.

I ended up buying them a new cage within a year. Actually, it's called an "animal environment". By using that phrase, you don't feel quite as insane about the amount of money you paid for it. It has a bottom that angles out to catch all droppings – food or otherwise. I've learned to be proud of the fact that my birds can stretch out further than that and still hit my dog on any three out of four attempts. When the cage was placed a whole room away from my carpet, they learned how to bomb the carpet during flight.

So every day I leave for work with the words, "I'm going now. I'll see you after work," as though they care. CB takes this as the signal to start eight fun filled hours of target practice on my dog. Captain interprets it to mean a long stretch of quiet time during which he can gauge which of my plants are guaranteed to break when he lands in them. And Mr. T just spends a lot of time trying to figure out why his back feels so warm and moist.

It's not your typical Arctic family group, but it's all mine!

Chapter 18

And the Winner is . . .

From the first day she came into my life, Lovey made it perfectly clear there'd be certain conditions placed on her stay with me. She expected the best seat in the car. She expected the sunniest spot in the room. She expected any and all dinner scraps. And when she gave me "the look", she expected me to understand that her position was non-negotiable.

If I wanted her to do something that was inconvenient to her plans, she shot me "the look". Some friends called it a sullen stare. Others likened it to the look of an animal born with limited intelligence. I knew better. I was being pointedly ignored. If I did try to move her along with some physical prompting – say two hands firmly shoving her butt – she would drop her not inconsiderable weight down to her ankles and in an instant become as immovable as Denali.

I didn't choose Lovey as my pet so much as she moved in and refused to leave. She was one of a litter of pups in town that could most charitably be called a very mixed breed. She showed up on my front porch one day not long before my wedding, walked in, sniffed dinner and decided she could be comfortable if I'd just keep the basic rules in mind. I'd return her to her rightful owners time and time again. In less than twenty-four hours, I'd find her sitting at my front door, tail wagging in anticipation of dinner.

When it became glaringly apparent that she'd made a decision about her future from which she would not be moved, I accepted the inevitable. I had the good grace to know when to surrender.

I initially tried to train her to be on a chain. She was not amused. I'd drag her outside to answer nature's call – an indignity she never quite accepted as a dog's lot in life – and clip the chain on. Then I'd tear back into the house. About ten minutes later, I'd cautiously peer out the window. Lovey would have her not insubstantial rear end planted firmly on the ground. The chain would be stretched out as tightly as possible with her head facing in its direction. She'd proceed to stretch her neck out until she was actually able to slip the collar off. This was not as hard as it sounds since her head seemed to shrink in proportion to the growth of the rest of her body.

Once free of the chain, she'd move about three inches and proceed with her business. It wasn't that she couldn't reach a good spot with the chain on. It was the principle of the thing.

When I moved into my Borough house, Lovey was ecstatic. At last, a home with central heat and carpeting. She quickly became a familiar sight in the neighborhood. I'd watch her head out every morning for her regular round of visits. She'd stop at various neighbors and scratch at the door. They'd open up and I'd see them put out scraps. Soon, she lost what little figure she'd once had and ballooned to a more than matronly size. The vet kept telling me how she was going to die young because she was so overweight. He kept telling me that for most of her seventeen years.

As her girth increased, she took on a somewhat Buddha-like attitude towards the world and its human inhabitants. Nothing was going to cause her to get upset or excited. Life was too short to not make it sweet. Somewhere in the depths of her overweight being she'd found her center and used it for balance.

I'd watch out the window as she crossed the street outside of the house. We were on a corner lot with a very busy four-way intersection right next to us. Lovey would go out when I got home from work. She'd retrace her morning rounds and head home about 6 p.m. There was still a lot of traffic then – though traffic is obviously being used in a Barrow sense here. There'd be skidoos, three wheelers, buses and cars all held up as Lovey made her slow, majestic progress across the intersection. Someone new to town might try honking. Most knew it was of no use. Honking just caused her to stop and look around to see who was being so rude and stupid. This merely prolonged the time it took her to cross.

One day, when she was around twelve years old, I came home and found her sleeping in the quanitchaq. I figured she and Sam had an argument while I was at work and she'd decided to wait outside for me. I figured a little nap in the Arctic winter was a good way to learn she shouldn't run away. Why I thought this would sink in then when it had never sunk in before has something to do with the incurable optimism I tend to have when it comes to my pets.

I wasn't really worried when she heaved her bulk up and started to limp into the house. She had arthritis and some hip dysphasia and I figured the cold had made her stiff. So long as she could still make it to the food bowl, I felt she'd survive whatever transient ache was bothering her.

By the next morning, Lovey was dragging around the house on her butt with her left back leg pointing straight up in the air. Even for Lovey this was strange behavior. What really cued me in to the seriousness of the situation, though, was her total disinterest in the hot dog I threw in the food bowl. For Lovey, this was the equivalent of needing CPR.

So I brought her to her favorite vet. Sure enough, she had somehow broken her leg. I can't say I was totally surprised. When you're about thirty pounds overweight – and you should only weigh forty pounds to begin with – you're risking a broken leg every time you chase after a car on an icy road. Since Lovey exhibited some characteristics of nearsightedness, she'd usually wait until the tire was about an inch from her nose before she'd jump up to chase it. Many a Barrow driver was startled to realize the tree stump by the side of the road was actually a dog capable of motion.

Lovey had her leg put in a cast. I found out quickly the functions a dog cannot perform with a cast. I had to grab her by the middle and pull her upright whenever she wanted to stand. This wasn't bad, though, since it was done in the privacy of our home. The only other witness was Sam and I knew far too much about him for him to risk a wise crack.

The other thing a dog cannot do with a back leg cast is squat to perform her daily functions. I had to follow her outside with a towel wrapped around her waist so I could support her while she did her thing. I hoped the Arctic night would help to hide what was happening. The remarks of varied and sundry friends and neighbors made it clear my hope was in vain.

But guilt is a great motivator when you've been raised a Catholic Italian. And despite my recovering Catholic status, the guilt remains an indelible part of my psychological make up. I had let her suffer an entire night before believing she was sick enough to bring to the vet. Clearly I was a terrible and negligent mother who was now being made to pay for her nonchalance.

Lovey did not age gracefully. She developed a digestive problem that – at its pinnacle – could empty a room in five seconds flat. I called it "terminal flatulence". The attack was frequently quiet and sneaky. We'd be sitting in the dining room playing bridge when the first wisps of odor would waft tentatively by. People would exchange startled looks as if not quite believing anything on earth could actually produce such a smell. Then they'd try to go back to the game. But it was a futile gesture. In less than a minute the second wave would hit. People would panic and run. Women and children would be trampled as Sam leapt over the couch heading for the door. Soon there'd be a crush of bodies attempting to squeeze through the doorway at one time. Wives would forget all love and loyalty to their husbands and beat on them to get through first. I once had my boss leap out of my car while it was still moving when Lovey laid one out during a drive.

The simplest way to describe the odor is to say it smelled as though Lovey were decaying from the inside out. And this was not the only lovely sign of aging she evinced. She went selectively deaf quite early. She also developed lovely bald spots on her chest, neck and certain selected leg joints. She developed a Ripley's "Believe It Or Not" case of dandruff. Then, in an unfortunate incident in the last year of her life, she lost all the hair from the end of her tail. She walked around with a tail that started out full and fluffy and then terminated abruptly in a rat-like little thing best hidden from sight.

It was during this period I entered her in a dog contest in Barrow. She was the hands-on favorite in the "Ugliest Dog" category. I knew she'd have no problem winning. What I never figured on was the standing ovation she'd receive when the announcement was made. Some of us are just born to be champs.

PARALLEL LOGIC

I can remember guests coming to my home in Lovey's later years – which started when she was about ten and went till she was seventeen. They'd catch a glimpse of her and exclaim, "Is that Lovey? She's still alive?" I could not quite figure out if they were referring to her condition in general or her motion at that specific moment.

Then there was the guest who watched as I stood about two feet behind Lovey shouting her name and tapping her on the shoulder to get her attention so she could go out. To accommodate her hip problems, I'd built a ramp for her personal use. I had the only house on the block that was modified for handicapped dog access.

Lovey stood immobile despite all my shouts. She never flinched, never turned her head or twitched her ear. I may have thought it was time to go out. She felt it was time for her fifth feeding. No use letting something out the back when there was still room inside for more.

My guest, in an awe-inspiring attempt to be polite, commented on how rarely it was you saw a dog that old alive. Though she didn't come right out and say it, there was the slightest question in her voice about keeping an animal alive who had so little brain function left. I hastened to assure her that though Lovey had grown a little slower with age – something most who knew her in her prime would not have thought possible – in actual fact her mental functioning was about where it had been all her life. That dazed expression had stood her in good stead for over seventeen years.

I can remember one night when she was laying on her back next to me as I wrote. She was wiggling like mad to scratch some itch. My Fit One exercise machine was next to her as she did this. Somehow, in the course of wiggling, she managed to hook one of her legs through an arm piece. This caused her to get stuck on her back, unable to roll to the right when she was ready for her nap. She lay there thinking about it for a moment. She whimpered slightly. Then she thought about it again, rolled to her left and fell asleep. She'd worry about unhooking her leg when she woke up. That is a dog with more mental functioning than most people I've ever known.

One night towards the end of Lovey's life, she had a pal come over for a visit. He was a few years younger than Lovey but at an age where those few years didn't make that much difference. Ekim was as old and set in his ways as she was. When together they truly did exist in parallel universes – side by side yet never quite touching. It was a comfortable friendship for them both

As I laid in bed reading, I glanced down at the side of the bed where Ekim and Lovey were curled up butt to butt. Ekim was chewing his paw in a rather desultory fashion. It was his version of an evening toilette. Lovey heaved and sighed as she folded her legs carefully to avoid the pain of her arthritis. She smacked her lips as she finally got comfortable and put her head down on her paws.

Once the two of them fell asleep, nuclear war wouldn't make them twitch. I can remember coming home from work to find them sound asleep at the front door. The noise of the garage door opening would not awaken them; the sound of my key in the lock didn't penetrate their consciousness; and the vibrations I created as I climbed over them to get into the living room did not register as even a tiny blip on their screens. When they slept, they slept as pros.

While they prepared to sleep off a hard day's napping, I heard the sound of ruffling feathers coming from the living room. My birds were also preparing to end their day. First though, as always, they would sit and chirp and coo together. They'd ruffle their feathers, lean their heads in to each other for a final grooming, fluff out their wings and in general act like two little old ladies from a bygone Victorian era preparing for their chaste but welcoming beds. No strange bodily sounds heard here. Except for when Captain is walking upside down inside his cage while weaving his head back and forth and making his eyes flash red, these are the aristocrats of my family.

When Lovey's legs went out the final time, I knew there was no hope for her. I knew what I had to do. It was possibly the hardest thing I've ever done. I held her till the end and sent her to my dad. I told her not to worry. He was the one who had taught me about the importance of food. He'd understand her needs. He'd keep her safe till I could join them both. It made it hurt a little less to know I could send her to someone with so much love to give.

A few days after she died, a little friend named Greta and I went to Lovey's grave. We stood there a few moments and said goodbye. Lovey had been Greta's best friend since birth. Despite the fact that Lovey was already quite old before Greta came into her life, they immediately bonded. I think Greta gave Lovey the kind of love and attention that kept her happily alive those last years. Greta is a loving child with instinctive sensitivity to animals. She knew, even at two, that Lovey was old and needed to be treated with gentleness. And with few exceptions, that was exactly how Greta treated her.

As we drove away from the grave, I was very silent. Greta, at seven, knew what the silence was about. She was quiet with me. After a few moments, she pointed to a cloud in the sky and said, "I think that's God's pillow". I muttered some form of assent. She persisted. "I think God lets Lovey sleep with him at night on that pillow". I looked at her and felt my first sense of comfort since Lovey's death. That day in the car, Greta was the grown up.

Within three days of Lovey's death, I had a new dog. The vets knew what the best cure was even if I wasn't very sure at first. They called to tell me they had a dog that had been sent up from one of our villages to be put to sleep. He was two years old and mostly needed someone with the patience to break some old habits and the love to overlook the rest. I went to the clinic with much hesitation. The feeling of disloyalty to Lovey was strong.

Then they put Mr. T in my arms. He'd just been shaved and was as scrawny and pathetic as they come. And – as the vets had rightly suspected – there was not a snowball's chance in hell I was going to hand him back and say, "No, I don't think so. Go ahead and kill him".

Mr. T – that stands for "testosterone" – is a pure bred miniature schnauzer. I've never owned a pure bred anything. I am much more comfortable with mutts. They're not quite so judgmental. I figure I have enough insecurity without feeling like I'm not meeting my dog's expectations.

But Mr. T seemed fairly upfront about his needs and wants. I was the servant, he was the master. It was quite clear and simple in his head. And in actual fact, this was probably the best thing that could have happened to me. He was so different from Lovey that I could love him without feeling disloyal to Lovey.

For instance, there's his odd and apparently insatiable appetite for dog chews and bones. He likes the glazed ones best. This way, he not only has the pleasure of the chew but also the fun of leaving reddish brown stains all over my carpet. By following them, I can pretty much reconstruct his daily path while I'm at work.

I buy the chews in large quantities for fear of running out. The few times I have, he's gotten pretty creative in what he's used as a substitute to satisfy his need to destroy something. He's already pretty much torn the underbelly out from my box spring. I think he was exploring its possibilities as a place to hide his various toys and treats from the big, bad mystery dog that comes looking for them while we sleep at night. I have found partially chewed, soggy rawhide bones in every nook and cranny in the house – to say nothing of underneath my pillow and in my boots.

I'm not sure if words can describe the feeling of sticking your foot in a boot in the morning and hitting something soft and soggy. If your coffee hasn't brought you fully awake, this surely will. Usually, though, he will bring the bone to bed at night and spend about ten minutes trying to push the covers over it while shoving it into the mattress. When he's done, about one eighth of an inch is covered, if any at all. But this somehow satisfies him that he can go out one last time without worrying about the safety of his family jewels. And I'm happy to know where the soggy mess is so I can put my boots on without fear in the morning.

Mr. T clearly realizes that being a miniature schnauzer in the Arctic has its drawbacks. Since the more typical Arctic dog outweighs him by five to six times his body weight, it's important to keep up a good front. As best I can tell, he tries to make up for his size in two ways.

For one, he acts like the fiercest creature on the planet. Woe betides the person foolish enough to enter my home to commit some nefarious deed – say, visiting or playing cards. He will greet you at the front door in such a fashion as to make absolutely clear you are now on his territory and he makes the rules.

Secondly, he tries to consume more chews, bones and box springs than any other animal in the world. This apparently helps keep his testosterone at a peak to overcome the negative effects of the neutering. Unfortunately, it hasn't shown the same positive effect on his intelligence.

For some reason, Mr. T has decided that one of his duties in life is to protect me from my birds. This is probably done less out of affection than as a reaction to a perceived threat to his food source. He clearly feels the birds are extraneous to happiness in our household and should therefore be eliminated. I do not share those feelings and have made that perfectly clear to him on more than one occasion. So he is frequently torn between his natural impulse to attack and his knowledge that said attack will be viewed dimly by the very person it's meant to protect.

You can see this knowledge lighting up a little bulb in his brain just about the time he's halfway across the linoleum and heading for the cage. Since the birds have only recently been moved onto the linoleum, the concept of fast stops on it still puzzles him. As the realization dawns that the attack is not a good idea, he plants his paws in front of him in an attempt to stop. He then slides head first into the plant stand next to the cage.

The plant stand, being made of solid wood and therefore slightly thicker than his skull, usually wins these encounters. I wait in vain for him to finally grasp that this will indeed happen every time he tries to stop on the linoleum. I thought sooner or later the pain of blasting into solid wood at 90 mph would teach him this was not a good idea.

This is not the only evidence I have that testosterone production is overtaking brain cell output. Mr. T loves to go out walking on the tundra. It's something we do almost every day. Unlike Lovey, he doesn't feel motion is a waste of energy better spent in eating or napping. In spring and summer, the tundra is full of birds. Mr. T thinks he has a better chance eliminating them than the parrot and cockatoo. So, he spends his walk time in futile attempts at cornering jaegers, snowy owls, and phalaropes.

Depending on the time of year, the birds will more or less tolerate his behavior. But if he gets too close to their nests, they attack with purpose. I'll be walking along enjoying the wonderful weather when I'll suddenly feel a quick breeze on my face. Seconds later a snowy owl is dive-bombing my dog, claws down and ready to grab. Mr. T usually has so much testosterone pounding in his ears from the excitement of possibly catching one of those birds, that he's unaware of the danger until I start frantically yanking his lead back. Then he looks up and gets a slightly quizzical expression on his face as it occurs to him that the flying creature above him not only outweighs him but also has bigger feet.

For most creatures this would be a humbling moment. Mr. T merely shrugs it off and starts pursuing lemmings instead. He's fairly confident at this point that most of them are smaller than he is. On most walks, he manages to miss every lemming near him. I've seen some run out from between his legs while he is nose deep in an empty lemming hole trying to figure out how there could be that much smell without something warm and furry attached to it.

Every once in a while, though, he accidentally catches one. What I find fascinating is how he will consistently come running back to proudly show me his kill. My reaction has never been one that would encourage a brighter animal to continue the activity.

Then he is forced to trot along with the lemming in his mouth looking for a place to bury it. The fact that he doesn't quite know what to do with it in no way means he's about to share or abandon it. It's his and he's keeping it whether it has any earthly use to him or not. Once again, he thinks with his hormones.

Eventually he finds a spot that for some reason looks better than the other fifty spots we've passed. He digs a somewhat smallish hole since tundra is not exactly easy to turn. But it's not the size that counts – it's the symbolism. We do this as often as necessary during the walk. It doesn't cause a problem until we start back.

He'll stop at each site and dig up his lemming. Then he trots along with it in his mouth until we come to the next grave. He drops the one in his mouth and digs the other one up. Then he looks at them both and panics. He'll pick one up, look down at the one left on the ground; drop the one in his mouth, pick up the one on the ground; look down at the first one, drop the one currently in his mouth – you get the idea. I am usually reduced to forcibly dragging him away before he goes crazy from indecision.

Mr. T is three years old now. We have many good years left to grow close. I hope I can survive them.

⦚ PARALLEL LOGIC ⦚

Chapter 19

Everyone's from somewhere else

Since most Alaskans are from somewhere else, we spend a lot of time visiting those places we came from and those friends we made in Alaska who have left the state. In my twenty-two years in the Arctic, I've seen a large number of people come and go. On their way in, their usual question is always "Why do you stay here?" On their way out, their usual question is, "Why do you stay here?" The basic answer is that it's a nice place to live.

I'm more than willing to trade off the weather and lack of shopping opportunities for the pleasure of living in a place that continues to fascinate and support, encourage and amuse me. I'm surrounded by people I like, many of whom are engaged in some fascinating activity like counting whales, studying traditional uses of plants and herbs or figuring out how to provide flush toilets at forty below.

But lots of people don't make a lifetime commitment to the Arctic and so every true Alaskan finds themselves at the airport saying good by more often than they'd like. After the first few teary scenes, I made a pledge to never go to the airport again. Then, after a few more painful farewells, I decided to be very selective about who could get close to me. Only people who were absolutely and irrevocably tied to the Arctic would be allowed the privilege. But all kinds of things can interfere with that resolve. Marriage, divorce, and illness – any one of these can undo a prior commitment to life amidst the snowy owls.

The other thing about friendships in the Alaskan Bush is that unless you are Alaska Native, you came from somewhere else. Friends become unbelievably close. They become the family we left behind. This way we have someone to eat Christmas dinner with and someone to split the drumstick with us on Thanksgiving.

When these friends leave, a gaping hole opens up in the fabric of our world. Saying goodbye is just not an option. My personal way to resolve this dilemma is to make very circuitous trips to the East Coast. I somehow convince myself that going to New Jersey via Dallas and Seattle is a relatively straight route. I alternate my trips so that each year as I travel east, I am routed through the home of a friend who has left the Arctic. It makes the good-byes at the airport a little less painful.

A definite upside to friendships in the Bush is fantasizing what kind of family your friends have as opposed to what your friends say about them. Every once in awhile, parents or siblings make a promise to visit while under the influence of some particularly sappy Andy William's Christmas scene, and you actually get a chance to see if the reality is anything like the stories. Sometimes, the family members appear on the scene and the resemblance between them and your friends is immediately obvious. They look alike, sound alike, and in some cases even dress alike (wasn't that once the theme of a Patty Duke show?). Other times, family members arrive and you find yourself wondering if your friend was adopted because the disparities are so great.

I always thought this was what would happen if my family came to visit. People would look at any one of my female relatives and wonder how those well dressed, sharp looking people could possibly be related to someone who thinks anything more than one pair of shoes in the closet at a time is unnecessary confusion.

Trying to explain Alaska to your family is hard enough. Trying to explain the Alaskan Bush to your family is damn near impossible. For years I struggled to find the words to describe the beauty of the Arctic – the hold it can exert on your psyche. All I got for my efforts were suggestions that the benefits of Prozac frequently outweighed the side effects. I finally gave up. There is no way to explain how that first blast of cold crisp air hitting you when the plane opens its doors in Anchorage is revitalizing to lungs made wimpy by that moist stuff they breathe in the lower '48.

Of course, there are always the cynics who feel obligated to point out that the air is apt to be cold and crisp even if it's July 28. There are those who will point out that cold, crisp air on July 28 is indicative of a very short tanning season – say, twenty minutes. To them I say, "Move to the tropics if you want the easy life". Here in Alaska, we thrive on adversity. With each passing year I spend in Alaska, I feel my character growing stronger because of its clearly superior ability to withstand any and all challenges hurled at me by my adopted state.

When friends and family in the lower '48 describe the horrors of their one measly blizzard per year, I respond with casual tales of going to work in weather of 40 degrees below with wind chills of 80 to 100 below and zero visibility due to wind gusts of 60 mph. I usually add something about ducking polar bears at the same time. I also make sure to note that I rarely let the weather cancel my daily racquetball game despite the fact that getting to it involves digging through fifty feet of solid snow and ice.

After all, what's the point of living through an Alaskan winter if you can't exaggerate at least a little?

Each year, when the sun goes down for the last time, I get calls from reporters wanting to know what we're going to do during the dark season. They clearly want some funny or startling anecdote about how the dark season makes every one go nuts. They want to hear how we hold some esoteric ritual to mark the last sunset for two months.

I'm always tempted to tell them we all strip our clothes off and go running around baying at the moon. But somehow it's never seemed appropriate. I'm afraid they won't get the joke.

I get the same kind of calls during the light season. And on the darkest day of the year. And the longest.

Just to put everyone's minds at ease, let me state categorically and unreservedly, "We do the same damn things during the dark season as we do during the rest of the year. We just use our lights more." Beyond that, there doesn't seem to be much more to say. But still the questions come. Do we have more babies after the dark season? How do we keep from going buggy without the sunlight? (Of course, that question makes an assumption not necessarily grounded in reality.)

Usually, about halfway through this kind of interview, my responses lead the reporters to suddenly grasp that not only is it dark, but the temperatures routinely run well below zero. Suddenly, a whole new sound of awe and respect creeps into their voices – the kind of respect you give to someone on the violently manic end of a manic-depressive problem.

In an effort to be kind, I tell them there is a definite upsurge in sales of tickets to Hawaii – Alaska's favorite beach. Then I mention that we have our Fourth of July fireworks during the dark season because they show up so much better. When asked if relationships break up more easily when it's dark, I tell them the only relationship I've had for years now involves a dog and two birds. I can't break up with them or I won't have a place to live. I don't know what people in relationships do.

Of course, when the sun comes back, someone will inevitably throw a "welcome-back-to-the-sun" party. But then, it doesn't really take much to give us an excuse to party. We've also been known to throw a "welcome to my parcel post package" party when the dark season starts to really annoy us.

The light season seems to bring less awe and mystery in its wake. People are able to handle the idea of 24-hour sunlight much better than they can handle the idea of 24-hour darkness. The only real question asked about it is how we sleep with the sun out all the time. I patiently explain that we in the Arctic are definite creatures of habit. If beds were good enough for the dark season, in all likelihood, that's how we'll sleep during the light season.

In the end, though, the concept of Alaska defeats a lot of people. No matter what you tell them, they are mystified. When dealing with Alaska, everything seems harder to them than it should. Retailers and merchants from the lower '48 are a prime example. They seem to feel that providing goods to Alaska should cost more. Sometimes it does. Sometimes they make it more expensive based on the idea that it must be. (Once again, parallel logic in the hands of amateurs is proven a dangerous weapon.) Basically, they treat Alaska like the dark side of the moon, where all natural laws of physics and earthly reality are suspended.

Let me give you an example. The "animal environment" I once bought for my birds came from California. One night, I decided to move it. I picked it up to lift it over a bump in the floor and it fell apart. Did I mention that it has no screws or nails – everything is held together by little plastic joints? As the cage collapsed, the birds took off in panicked flight, bombing everything they passed. My dog ran in mad circles barking and trying to protect his forty-three chew toys at once. I stood there holding the remains of the cage in my arms thinking there had to be a better life somewhere.

For reasons too insane to get into now, I ended up accidentally super gluing the door shut when I put the cage back together. This meant I had to break it to let the birds get in to their food and water. This further meant I had to call the company in California from whom I purchased it to ask for more of the little plastic joints.

They were extremely helpful and courteous. They would be happy to send me some and would even do so free of charge. Why they were so nice, they even said they'd throw a few extra in the bag just in case. I was thrilled at the fast and efficient response. I hung up the phone with a little glow at the basic humanity of most salespeople.

About thirty seconds later, the phone rang again. It seems they hadn't noticed my address was in Alaska. There would be a small handling charge and they needed my permission to put it on my credit card. The glow dimmed a little but I figured they were already providing me the joints for free. I couldn't complain if they wanted to break even on the shipping.

One week later, I received an envelope in the mail. It had a 29-cent stamp on it. Inside were my "free" plastic joints. A month later, I got my credit card statement. It had a $12 handling charge on it. I went home and tried to think calmly. Exactly what had they done for me – what extra cost had they incurred – in putting those plastic joints in a envelope with a 29-cent stamp that they would not have incurred in serving a customer from Sandusky, Ohio.

Absolutely nothing! I had just been zapped with the Alaska factor. If it was being mailed to Alaska, it had to be more difficult no matter what reality seemed to indicate.

I called the company back and chatted with them about this concept. They agreed it did seem absurd and said they'd remove the charge from my credit card.

They never did. So I called them back and we chatted some more. This time they said they could only remove nine dollars of the charge. Why? Well, because I lived in Alaska and there was an extra charge for sending things here. They apparently felt that was more than ample justification.

I wasn't surprised. They weren't the only ones who felt that way. I called to have some popcorn sent to me from a catalogue I'd received in the mail. I made the mistake of assuming that if they mailed catalogues to Alaska, they would have the ability to handle an order from here. I was right. They could handle an order from here. They couldn't handle the concept that we were a full partner in the union of states we call America and received the US mail with about the same efficiency. In fact, since the days planes started taking over for dog teams in mail delivery, our wait time has gotten shorter and shorter till its almost normal.

After placing my order for popcorn, I heard those words I've come to dread, "Oh wait a minute, you're from Alaska, aren't you? I have to check with my supervisor about special mailing instructions." She came back on the line about thirty seconds later and announced that the cost to ship to Alaska would be a bit higher than listed in the catalog since it would have to come second day UPS express. I suggested that I really didn't need to have the popcorn delivered that quickly and asked how it was shipped in the lower '48. Not at all to my surprise, it went out in the good old US mail. I asked for the same service and told the salesperson I would accept any responsibility if it didn't show up still hot from the pot. She told me that was not an option. UPS had the contract for Alaska and everything went through them and they sent it second day express.

That cost almost doubled the cost of the order. I canceled it.

This was not my first encounter with UPS second day delivery. They got to my mother too. Mom has made it a practice to send me a package every Christmas. This practice started in the days when precious little was available locally. She stocked me up on various pastas and olive oils and hunks of grating cheese. And then she always threw in interesting extras. Over time, everyone in the family contributed to the holiday box. Anyone wanting to send something north for me would add it to the mélange prepared by mom.

Sometimes the contents have been a little startling. They resemble the contents you would box up to send to someone living in a foreign country that also qualified as a Third World nation. For instance, sugar free gelatins and packaged corn muffin mixes often made up a good deal of the box's bulk.

But more startling than the occasional bar of soap is the mystery that surrounds mailing the box to me. After all these years, it still seems more difficult than it should be – once again, the mystique of Alaska defeats the reality of Alaska.

Mom always mailed the package to me through parcel post. Although this took about six weeks, it had never been a problem for me since the packaged mixes were usually not due to expire until the next millennium. But one year, for some unknown reason, mom decided to go with UPS on the theory I would get it while the muffin mixes were still fresh.

After mailing the package, she called to tell me it was on the way. Then she added that it would be the last time she ever did this due to the exorbitant price increase in mailing. Being a dutiful daughter, I thoughtfully queried, "What exorbitant price increase?" She told me the dollar amount and I came unglued. Suddenly the items in the package could have been bought cheaper at the tip of the Aleutian chain. Since I was unaware of any crises that could have precipitated such a price increase at either the Post Office or UPS, I awaited the package with some interest to see just what she had paid for.

What she had paid for – I found out five days later when it arrived – was 2nd day express service. What you have to understand here is that I'm dealing with a woman who will stay up until 11 p.m. in order to call me for a few cents less per minute. She will yawn through the entire call and often be barely coherent. But the idea of calling on anything less than the late night rates makes her crazy. Yet she sent the package 2nd day express because she was sure it was the only way to get it here before the gelatin expired.

There is a political party here in Alaska devoted to the idea of Alaskan independence. It's one of those "fringe" parties that engender more laughter than respect in most parts of America. But here in Alaska, its message is beginning to be more and more appealing. If we're going to be treated like a foreign country, then let's be one. I hear the reporting requirements for foreign aid are far less exacting than for federal grants.

Chapter 20

We are not barren . . .

One of the most annoying things about living in the Arctic is reading or hearing about your home in the news. The lead into any story about the Arctic usually carries the words "wind swept and barren" within the first paragraph. I've almost come to believe it's some unwritten rule of journalism. If you're going to mention the Arctic, be sure to say its wind swept and barren.

Well, I might concede the wind swept part – especially on those days when the gusts are hitting ninety miles per hour. I can remember going out in a storm like that on the mistaken assumption that if my car couldn't make it through the drifts and blowing snow, I could. I was due on the radio and the only DJ who'd been able to get to the station that morning was desperate for some relief. I'd walked – and I use that term quite loosely here – about two blocks when I found myself up to my waist in a snowdrift. I could neither go forward nor easily turn back. A gust of wind came along that picked up my not inconsiderable girth, lifted me fully in the air and turned me completely around. When I touched ground again I was facing in the direction from which I'd come.

I took this as a sign from God and fought my way back to my house. The four-block round trip took over an hour. The friend who had started out with me – in fact, she was the one who had the bright idea we could make it across town on foot if the car couldn't get through – insisted on continuing forward after I turned back. She crawled into her house about two hours later, one minute before we sent Search and Rescue out for her.

After she thawed and caught her breath, she described the gust of wind that came along and blew her across the road, through a few drifts and on towards the lagoon. She managed to grab a telephone pole or she would still be tumbling along like that proverbial tumbling weed. When she felt brave enough to let go of the pole, she fell to her hands and knees and crawled back to her house. She figured this was the only way to get out of the wind enough to make any headway.

The DJ on the radio ended up there most of the day since no one else could get through. The only reason he made it was because he only lived half a block from the station.

The wind here is quite a demanding element. It can take a temperature of minus 10 degrees and plummet it down to 65 below with wind chill. You walk to the store with the wind at your back and think, "This isn't so bad". Then you turn around to come home and frostbite your nose in the first twenty feet.

Even in the summer when it doesn't blow quite as cold, it still can be a factor in all activities. Once, a roommate of mine named Terry decided to build a traditional kayak. He wandered the town asking advice from the older men. Since he was non-native, some of the men saw a lot of humor in his attempts to re-create a skin kayak. They were laughing because as he asked their advice, they were preparing their aluminum, factory made skiffs to go out hunting.

Eventually he succeeded in his task right down to the sealskins that he had personally hand sewn for the cover of the kayak. Now it was time to try it out. We went down to the beach for the initial launch and immediately attracted quite a crowd. It was a perfect summer night in the Arctic. The sun was rolling along the horizon over the ocean, the wind was blowing enough to keep the mosquitoes at bay and the water was ice free and relatively calm.

Terry went out first and it was a smashing success. Smashing success is defined here as neither sinking nor taking on so much water it looked like a floating aquarium. The only real problem was that the paddle cracked in the middle. A kayak has only one paddle. It's flattened on both ends so that you row by dipping each end in the water alternately. Terry had only made one paddle. He came back to shore and it was now my turn to hop in. I was a little nervous about the broken paddle but Terry assured me that all I had to do was hold it in the middle where the crack was and it was perfectly functional. Being young and foolish, I believed him. My pride was also on the line. A large crowd had now gathered. I was determined to show them I could handle this.

I carefully got in the kayak and Terry pushed me out towards the sun and horizon. A friend of mine who had a camera took pictures of me as I paddled away. It was a stunning scene. I was silhouetted against the sun while I paddled on water with a golden tinge. The sun sent out a ray that played across the water like a brilliant carpet lay out before me to show me the way. The photos, when developed, were everything any photographer could ask for – perfect composition, perfect light – you couldn't have made these pictures better if you painted them.

Fortunately, they did not show the panic occurring on the kayak as I realized the wind was blowing me straight towards the sun and the Soviet Union and I had absolutely no control because of the broken paddle. What started out as fun ended up as an hour of hysterical attempts to turn the kayak around and get back to shore. Unfortunately, those on shore could not tell what the problem was since my back was to them. I couldn't turn around and shout it out because I risked flipping the kayak. All I could do was listen to their shouts of "That's far enough." "Turn around now." "You're going too far out." "There could be whales out there, be careful!"

Eventually I turned the kayak around and paddled back into the wind. I made it to shore through sheer will power and panic. By the time I got back on land, I was soaking wet from perspiration and fear. I'd had visions of blowing clear to Siberia. Better yet, I'd had visions of being up-ended by a breaching whale and getting to play out some modern day version of "Jonah and the Whale".

Terry, who still insisted the craft was eminently maneuverable if handled properly (and preferably with a paddle that wasn't cracked in the middle), would later be rescued by a ship while drifting off shore from Point Barrow also heading towards the Soviet Union.

Getting back to the point of this story – the Arctic is windswept. I'll concede that point. But the barren part still makes me nuts.

Here is a land filled with animals, plants and people – in fact, parts of the Alaskan Arctic contain some of the last unspoiled wilderness in the world. This is not a barren land. Reporters who describe it as such show that they are too lazy to do their homework or have a blatant disregard for the truth.

Living in the Arctic is certainly a challenge. It's one made a little harder by the weather and a little easier by the people. The Inupiat of the North Slope are people who have been tempered by the harshness of the climate and gentled by the beauty of their land. They have faced cultural genocide – whether deliberate or not – and have stared it down. They are the first group of Native Americans who have so successfully used the institutions of the western world to protect their cultural heritage.

The North Slope Borough is, if you think about it for a moment, quite a bold and brave experiment. It came about because of the wisdom of our local leaders at a time when the development of Prudhoe Bay could have truly finished off what measles and TB epidemics started.

It is the conceit of western civilization to believe that we are superior in all ways to all other cultures that ever existed in this world. Although the phrase Eurocentric has become a politically correct joke among intellectuals of all persuasions, living in an indigenous American culture brings Eurocentricity right into your face.

On one of my first trips back east after I moved to Barrow, my friend Sandra accompanied me. She already had some experience traveling outside of Barrow since she'd gone to Hawaii with some teachers as a baby sitter.

In order to travel East with me, she needed to make enough money for her plane ticket. I told her I would cover all expenses once we got there. Sandra was young and healthy despite the fact that she occasionally smoked cigarettes. So she decided she'd make her plane fare by winning the Fourth of July Marathon. That, added to some savings she already had, would put her over the top.

Her idea of training for the marathon was to stop smoking at least ten minutes before the race began. The length of the race was not quite Olympic but did involve at least five miles. The depth of her determination to win can be gauged by the fact that she took first place despite not having trained for it at all. Being sixteen probably had something to do with it too.

When she crossed the finish line, her legs were shaking so bad she went down like a sack of potatoes. Her boyfriend had to literally pick her up and carry her to my couch because she couldn't walk. Before he carried her off, however, she stopped by the judges and picked up her money.

I thought it would be fun to surprise my mother with my visit home that year so I didn't tell her I was coming. In retrospect, this was not the brightest thing to do when traveling thousands of miles with an unexpected guest in tow. I can still picture our ascent up the stairs to my folk's place. Sandra was walking behind me. I rang the bell and a face looked down over the banister. As we headed up the stairs, this face – which happened to belong to mom – looked down and said, "Can I help you?" in a very polite and impersonal tone. I realized she didn't recognize me.

On the best of days, an occurrence like this will throw you. But on that particular day, I had a sixteen-year-old walking behind me whom I'd dragged across an entire continent to meet my family. And now, here I was walking into what I claimed to be my childhood home and my mother didn't recognize me. Mom would later claim that she was wondering who this person was who looked so much like her daughter. Apparently I didn't resemble her daughter enough to trip any memory wires in her head.

There is probably some intriguing psychosis involved with that whole exchange that I choose to ignore for fear the truth will heal me. Or, it's proof positive of the fact that parallel logic is a genetic inheritance.

After we'd straightened out the mix up over my identity, the visit proceeded rather smoothly. Sandra was clearly enjoying the insanity that is an Italian family up close and personal and I was having a ball showing her around the East Coast. Since Sandra was a mature sixteen, I often forgot how young she really was and treated her as an adult. Then we'd do something like taking a ride on the New York City subway system. I would be swiftly reminded of how young she was and how strange and frightening a big city can be to someone brought up in a town of 2800.

I had first run into this phenomenon in Barrow. I'd be talking to a patient about going out to Anchorage for further tests and they'd allow as how they'd never been out of Barrow before and were a little nervous. We'd get to talking and I'd realize that except for the occasional movie or TV show, some of my patients had never actually seen a sidewalk or traffic light. They'd never touched a tree or walked barefoot in grass. Neon signs, pavement, brick buildings – hell, a building over two stories high – were all as foreign to them as the dark side of the moon.

Because of all the changes in Barrow since the formation of the Borough and the development at Prudhoe Bay, you don't find people like this anymore in Barrow. Everyone has had a chance to go to Fairbanks or Anchorage through school trips or family visits. Now that employment is available and planes come in more often than three times a week, people are not as isolated.

Sandra had been outside of Barrow before her trip home with me but never to a big crowded city like New York. So when I announced we would be taking the subway from my friend's apartment in Brooklyn to Manhattan, I automatically went into a lecture on what to do if we got separated. I explained that sometimes the trains were really crowded and people pushed and shoved.

Should we get separated, I explained, all she had to do was find a cop or a phone. If she found a phone she was to call my friend Barbara at work and Barbara would talk her back to Brooklyn. Should she find a cop first, she was to throw herself on his mercy, explaining that she was a little lost Eskimo (go for the sympathy vote when it will help!), and would he help her get back to her friends. I hesitated to suggest she try a taxi since convincing a taxi to go to Brooklyn from Manhattan is a chore best left to the hardened and experienced.

I still vividly remember one of my first attempts to convince a cabby that he had to take me to Brooklyn no matter what his personal feelings on the matter were. I got in and gave him my destination. He reacted as though hit by a poisoned dart. I refused his barely civil request to get out and find another cab. Being young and naive, I thought I'd impress him with the fact that if he refused I'd make him drive me to the first cop so I could report his refusal and get him in trouble. This is not a wise statement to make to a man operating a piece of heavy, moving machinery in which you are but a passenger.

We tore off down the street peeling rubber as we went. Since I was still too stupid to realize just how annoyed this man was, I further exacerbated the situation by insisting he take the Brooklyn Bridge since it was nearest to my destination. I also thought it important to point out the fastest route to the bridge from the bus terminal. As I look back on the situation now, even I am amazed by the level of arrogant ignorance I was exhibiting – or maybe it was just a thinly veiled death wish.

We hit the highway leading to the bridge doing about 90. We were in the far left lane of a four-lane highway. The exit for the bridge was on the right. As we zoomed past it, I tapped the driver on the shoulder and sweetly pointed out his error. I might also have made a comment on how I was no hick new to town. If he tried to take me out of my way to get extra fare, I wouldn't pay it. This again was not a bright statement to make to someone who has his life in your hands.

He hit the brakes and brought the cab to a screeching halt. Then he backed up into oncoming traffic while simultaneously cutting across the four lanes. We made it to the bridge exit one second short of my decorating the back of his cab with my latest meal. This was not the kind of experience I wanted Sandra to have. So I never mentioned cabs as a means of transportation. I told her they were there merely as street decorations – to add ambiance to the feel and smell of the city.

Sandra listened to my instructions on emergency measures to take if we were separated and then took a grip on my elbow that has left visible fingerprints even today, almost twenty years later. If by any chance we did get separated, my arm would be going with her no matter where the rest of my body ended up.

Later in that visit, I took Sandra to the beach in Atlantic City. Having been raised by the shore, the water and waves were old friends. Sandra had also been raised by the shore – only in her case it had been the shore of the Arctic Ocean. The Arctic is an ocean you swim in for only two purposes.

One is to join the Polar Bear Club. This is a group of semi-sane individuals who jump in the ocean in Barrow in August when the ice has cleared enough for open water to be accessible from shore. To legitimately join, you actually have to put your head under the water.

There is no way to describe the sensation of frigid water hitting your body as you dive into the Arctic. There are fewer ways to describe what it does to your body. For men, in particular, this can be an interesting experience. Certain parts of their sexual organs attempt to retreat back into the body in protest. The good news is that they do return after a reasonable amount of time.

Another problem is that you can't really feel what's happening as the cold causes your body to get numb. This would explain one potential club member's embarrassing exit from the water. He had swum out a little distance to show just how hardy he really was. When it came time to turn back, he stood up and walked in from the sea. A large crowd stood on the beach watching the event.

Later, the erstwhile club member would admit that he thought it was harder than it should have been to walk out but he thought it was just the water impeding his progress. He would have continued thinking that had it not been for the roar of laughter exploding from the beach coupled with the fact that the water was now well below his knees and his steps still felt impeded.

He glanced down only to find his swimsuit around his ankles. Public nudity is uncomfortable for most people most of the time. Public nudity at a time when you greatest treasures are at their smallest moment – well, its incidents like this that keeps counselors and liquor stores busy.

The only other reason for swimming in the Arctic Ocean is if you've fallen in from a boat. Then you swim like a bat out of hell because you have a very small window of time to save yourself before you freeze to death.

Based on these facts, Sandra was not at all sure about the joys of swimming in the Atlantic with waves crashing all about. So she took another grip on my elbow that made it clear we would sink or swim together. Luckily, we swam!

Sandra and I had a great time on that vacation. But the moment that sticks out the most clearly in my mind is one involving a wonderful person named Rocco Pestilli – Grandpop Roc. Grandpop came to this country from Italy many, many years ago. He brought nothing with him except a desire for a better life and hands that could work wonders with stone.

His was the typical turn-of-the-century European immigrant story. He worked hard and long, became known for his skill, integrity and charming personality, and eventually ended up with his piece of the American dream – a home in the suburbs, a car in the garage and a garden in his back yard.

PARALLEL LOGIC

The day Sandra and I arrived on the East Coast, we rented a car from Kennedy Airport and drove to Philadelphia. I don't remember why we drove there instead of going straight to Atlantic City. I might have thought that mom and dad were visiting there for the day. I have many relatives in the Philadelphia area, most of whom live in a suburb called Glenside.

In one of those strange occurrences for which there is no natural cause, almost every one from the old neighborhood in Nicetown – a section of northwest Philly – moved to the same ten-block radius in Glenside when the city took their land for an expressway. I found myself driving from one house to the next looking for signs of life. No one was home anywhere we went.

We finally ended up in Grandpop Roc's back yard where he was having lunch with some friends. In all his years in America, he'd never really lost his accent. In fact, as often seems to happen with many immigrants, as he aged his ability to speak English actually seemed to diminish and his Italian became more pronounced.

Sandra was standing beside me as I asked where all the family was. It turned out they were all in Atlantic City for the day. I thanked him for the information and then turned to introduce him to Sandra before getting back in the car for the next two-hour leg of the trip. As I made the introduction, the thought crossed my head that here indeed was the meeting of the old and the new in America. Sandra's family had been in this country since time immemorial. Grandpop had just laid down his roots for his family to claim this new country as their own. It was polar opposites meeting. The complete history of this country laid between them.

And then I heard Grandpop say – with enormous pride in his voice and an accent it would have taken a saw to hack through – "Welcome to my country!" I looked at Sandra and for just a brief moment I understood how thoroughly we had displaced the people to whom this continent really belonged.

Living with the people of the Arctic has taught me new depths to the meaning of patience and tolerance. And it's taught me that paradise is where you make it – even in the windswept, barren Alaskan Arctic!

About the Author . . .

Elise Sereni Patkotak was born into a much kinder and gentler world. Her initial view of life was bounded by the Italian immigrant neighborhood in Atlantic City, New Jersey in which she was raised and the nuns who taught her throughout her early years. She is now a recovering Catholic.

Elise lived in Barrow, Alaska for 28 years during which time she aged with astounding rapidity. During her time in Barrow, she was a nurse, health director, social worker, columnist, radio show host, public information officer, city recreation director and Guardian Ad Litem. She now lives in Anchorage with five parrots, a cockatoo and two mutts who will sell all her secrets for a treat.

Elise has a small writing/graphics company, Precious Cargo, Ltd. that she hopes will actually turn a profit before she dies. She does freelance writing in her spare time to pay for her annual trip to a Third World country where she assists her sister in personally trying to raise their GNP for that year. Her primary goal in life is to live long enough to spend all she has saved for her old age.

PARALLEL LOGIC